MEDIUM RARE

MEDIUM RARE

The Biography of Liam Scott

LIAM SCOTT
WITH BILLY ROBERTS

APEX PUBLISHING LTD

First published in 2009 by
Apex Publishing Ltd
PO Box 7086, Clacton on Sea, Essex, CO15 5WN

www.apexpublishing.co.uk

British Library Cataloguing-in-Publication Data
A catalogue record for this book
is available from the British Library

ISBN   1-906358-49-4   978-1-906358-49-5

Typeset in 11.5pt Times New Roman

Production Manager: Chris Cowlin

Typeset by: Craig Kay

Cover Design: Siobhan Smith (Photo: John Morosoni Whelan)

Printed by the MPG Books Group in the UK

From Liam Scott:
I dedicate this book to my mum 'Kate'. Hope you like it?

Contents

Foreword by Lynsey de Paul   vi

Introduction   vii

Chapter One: The Early Years in Dublin   1

Chapter Two: A New Beginning in England   7

Chapter Three: Becoming a Man and a Criminal   15

Chapter Four: Moving On   26

Chapter Five: Sailing Close to the Wind: 36

Chapter Six: In the Hands of Angels   44

Chapter Seven: Never Go Back to Where You've Already Been   50

Chapter Eight: The Powers of the Mind   58

Chapter Nine: A Thousand Mile Journey Begins With a Single Step   63

Chapter Ten: The Actor and the Medium   71

Chapter Eleven: Old Habits Die Hard   78

Chapter Twelve: Light on the Distant Horizon   80

Chapter Thirteen: The Universe Smiles at Me   89

Chapter Fourteen: From Rags to Riches, Riches to Rags   94

Chapter Fifteen: Philosophically Reviewing My Life   103

Chapter Sixteen: Spiritual Development and Me   110

Conclusion   115

Foreword

by Lynsey de Paul

It is said that we may have multiple lives and that there is such a thing as reincarnation. However, some of us have many incarnations within one life. Such a person is Liam Scott.

I first met Liam over twenty years ago in his building incarnation when his company put back the steeple and weather vane on top of my Gothic house, which 'went west' in the 1987 gales around the UK. From what I gather, he had had a somewhat 'colourful' career before that.

He was always a little larger than life, generous and thoughtful with a gentle heart inside a bear of a man. I witnessed his metamorphosis into healing and clairvoyance.

It is fascinating to watch Liam in action in front of an audience that he continually surprises with his gift of uncannily knowing certain facts about them, while bringing messages from those they have known in the past.

This is the story of his lives.

Lynsey de Paul

Introduction

Liam Scott's colourful life has most certainly taken many turns during his seventy-two years on this planet. 'Character building turns', Liam says proudly, in his easy-to- listen to Cockney drawl, that makes him the man he is today – likeable, charismatic, strong and very relaxed. Although Liam is frequently mistaken for American crooner Tony Bennet, 'any similarity stops there', he jokes, although he is fanatical about Jazz, and uses his favourite Jazz records to help him unwind at the end of a long and very hard day. When Liam Scott landed in the UK from Dublin during World War Two at the age of nine, circumstances forced him to grow up fast, and he quickly learned to defend himself on the rough streets of North London. After Liam's father was killed in Burma during the war, his mother moved with her three children to London, where they lived with family at their home in Islington. Although life here in England was completely different to life in Ireland, Liam loved it and settled in quickly to his new school, Saint John the Evangelist. Liam was devastated when the council re-housed the family, and relocated them in Tottenham. From then on the young Liam found it difficult to settle, and by the age of thirteen he had developed a bad stutter, and was forever being taunted by the other kids. The stutter combined with his broad Irish brogue, made him a target for every playground bully. However, through sheer strength and determination, he overcame this nervous infliction, and the brave young Liam soon proved himself to be tough and able to stand up in any confrontational situation. He soon won the respect of the other kids and was then able to walk with the toughest of those struggling to survive in war-torn North London.

After serving his obligatory two years army conscription during the 1950s, Liam's streetwise attitude helped him to duck and dive in gangland London, earning him the respect of some of the toughest men on the streets. From a very early age he seemed to have an aptitude for making money, and with a finger in many different pies, he created a nice life for himself and his family. Even today, although Liam lives a very different life to the one he lived even thirty years ago, he has an air about him that he has done and seen it all. Those who know him know him to be a deep thinker, and most certainly a man of mystery. In fact, I think it's only fair to say that you have to be in his company for some time to realise that there is far more to him than a flash, well-dressed man with cockney mischief in his eyes. Although I have known him for some years, I have only met him on a few occasions. It is only through writing this book that I have come to realise just how much he actually has to offer.

Most people who really know Liam Scott, know him to be softhearted and extremely good natured. But they also know there is a line that nobody can cross. He is a private man, and a very deep thinker. He is also quite eloquent when expressing his point of view, and has deep, philosophical opinions about life and even death. Although I have known Liam Scott for a few years now, over the last six months I have come to see him in a completely different light. His mediumistic skills transcend just giving messages from the so-called 'other side' of life. He possesses an inherent, profound belief in the spiritual evolution of mankind, and just being in his presence one is overwhelmed by this. Liam Scott is a philosopher and, in my opinion, a man born out of his time. He is one of life's silent observers, but never passes judgement on anyone.

Liam is the first to admit that he was a bit of a villain in earlier times, and a complete contrast to the man he is today. He frequently socialised with the Kray brothers and, although then a fairly young man, was accepted as one of the 'Firm', the name used to designate the notorious followers of the infamous twins. Gradually Liam Scott won the respect of most of the criminal fraternity in London, and was regarded by many as 'friend'. It was soon clear to Liam that he had the ability to make money from anything, and slowly established various legitimate businesses, from which he eventually became an extremely wealthy man. Although most of his money was made from his very lucrative scrap-metal business, he also had a successful second-hand car business. In fact, for some years it seemed that he had the Midas touch where his business acumen was concerned, and he used this by exploiting every opportunity that came along. Liam always had an eye for the main chance, and was known by his peers to be extremely fair, and yet very ruthless in business. He has always possessed an inherent, Celtic intuitive skill, and has always used this when making decisions involving business deals of one kind or another.

But Liam's comfortable life was to come tumbling down around him, and he lost all his money. His life had taken yet another turn, and although not completely penniless, circumstances had forced him to start all over again. He occasionally reflects nostalgically on his life and finds it difficult to believe some of the things he has done in the seventy-two years he has lived. Little did Liam realise in those days, that one of the Kray's oldest friends, Laurie O'Leary, also theatrical agent and impresario, would one day manage the famous medium, Doris Stokes. Although now deceased, Liam speaks fondly of Laurie O'Leary, the man he had known for many years, and says nostalgically that he was often mistaken for Laurie. Whilst compiling the material for this book, I asked him would he change anything in his life if he had it to live all over again. His answer quite surprised me. 'Not one thing!' he said, firmly, a glint of nostalgia in his eyes. 'I'd probably do it all over again. It's all been good fun. Dangerous, but good fun!' I think that's part of what makes Liam Scott the man he is today. One thing is certain, had he been told when he was a young man, that one day he would be working as a medium, he would never have believed it. Nonetheless, today Liam Scott is an extraordinary medium, and a man with exceptional qualities. In fact, he is truly a 'Medium Rare', living a life that is far from over.

Chapter One
The Early Years in Dublin

I was born on the 26th November 1935 at 6am in Dublin, Ireland, to my parents, Alexandra and Kathleen Scott. Although my entrance into this world was fairly uneventful, I was the first born, and the baby boy my parents so badly wanted. When I was born, my father was in the Irish army, and my mother was struggling to make ends meet. At this time we lived in a second-floor flat in Dorset Street, Dublin, and although we had very little in the way of furniture, it was home to me. Our family lived a fairly simple life, and although money was quite scarce, I was loved and wanted for nothing. As far as I can recall, my father was an extremely restless man, and when I was around the age of four he deserted the army. By then my brother Sean had been born, and although I was only four, I was made to feel quite grown-up and in charge of my baby brother. The night the Red Caps came looking for my father, it was cold and raining heavily. Dad told me to say that I hadn't seen him, before climbing out onto the window-ledge to hide from them. The two military policemen searched the flat from top to bottom, and I can remember my heart beating heavily inside my chest, in case they looked through the window and saw my dad out there on the

1

window-ledge, hiding from them in the pouring rain. Once they were satisfied my father wasn't there, they left. My mother then gave my dad the all clear, and he climbed back in through the window. For some months he had to keep his head down, and although the Red Caps called to the flat several times looking for him, he always managed to avoid being caught. When I was five my sister, Kathy, was born. Then I really did feel grown-up and in charge. Even at the age of five I was a very inquisitive child with no sense of danger. One afternoon I wandered from the flat and found my way to a nearby railway embankment. I stumbled heavily and fell all the way down the grassy slope onto the railway lines. Fortunately, the lines onto which I had fallen were not very busy, and so I escaped with minor cuts and bruisers. My father went berserk and shouted at my mother for allowing me out of her sight.

When I was eight my dad joined the British Army, the Lancashire Fusiliers. My mother told me that he did this because he wanted to fight in the war. Dad was like that! He apparently wanted desperately to do his bit for King and country. At that time we had been staying with my dad's mother at her pub in County Cork. Although I loved my gran, she was a very strange woman who always wore a cap on her head and a woollen shawl around her shoulders. The day my dad left for Burma, he took me for a walk down a nearby country lane. He had my little brother, Sean, on his shoulders and he held my hand as we walked. It was a beautiful autumnal afternoon, and the birds were singing happily because it was quite warm and the sun was shining. 'You won't be seeing me for some time!' he said, softly. 'I want you to look after your mother, Kathy and Sean while I'm away.' I felt sad but so proud that my dad had asked me to look after the family. I felt sort of grown-up and in charge. I didn't know it then but that was to be the last time I would see my father. He was killed in Burma in 1944. I can remember the day the postman delivered the telegram informing my mother that my father had been killed in action. She was understandably devastated, and I didn't know what to do. I remembered my father's last words, 'Look after your mother, Kathy and Sean.' I knew then I had to be strong, because I had to take my dad's place and look after the family. Although there was no funeral for my father, my mother went out and bought herself a black outfit, which she wore for a couple of weeks, mourning my dad. Looking back, it was quite sad really. My mother loved my father very much, and I didn't think she would cope without him. However, my mother was of strong stock, and could be quite stern and very hard. She was extremely resilient and determined to survive, if only for the sake of her children.

Although I tried desperately to be grown-up, I was still only eight years old. Since dad had gone, our family somehow did not feel the same. My mother used to go out a lot and leave me to look after my young brother and sister. I seemed to always feel quite miserable and desperately wanted it to be better. Eventually my mother took us to stay with her mother, Grandma Helen, while she went to work in a factory in England. Granny was a nice lady but very religious and superstitious. She was always talking about banshees and fairies. Looking back I can now see that this was an integral part of Irish tradition and folklore, and granny believed in all that sort of stuff. Although I had always had what I suppose you could call 'second sight', Grandma Helen made me aware of other things, such as banshees and the spirits of our dead ancestors. Every 31st October, on All Souls Day, or Halloween as it is also called, Granny Helen would light a roaring peat fire, and then back it up with logs and peat from a nearby farm. I used to see all sorts of faces in the flames of the fire as they roared up the chimney. I would sit, mesmerised by the things I could see, and Granny would watch me thoughtfully, smiling to herself. She obviously knew what I was looking at, and also knew that I had some sort of second sight, just like her. Once we were undressed and ready for bed, she would place some apples in a bucket of water and let us duck our heads into it to see how many we could retrieve in our mouths. It was great fun and made Halloween a real 'Duck Apple Night'. Before we retired for the night, Granny Helen would back the fire with more peat and logs, making sure that the flames would roar through the night, and then she would place several plates of cakes and slices of meat and a couple of jugs of milk on the table. The table would always look as though it was laid for a feast. She also made sure that there was a bowl of hot water, a few bars of soap and some clean towels. 'The food is for the souls of our dead ancestors',

4

she would say, a serious look on her face. 'The water and soap is for them to wash themselves, and the fire is to warm them before their journey to wherever they are going!' Although it all intrigued me, that night I would sleep with my head beneath the sheets, scared to look into the shadows in the corner of my room, just in case I saw something I didn't want to see. It's funny, but I would always hear a dog howling and would think it was a banshee coming with the souls of my dead ancestors to eat at Granny's table. I would lie there for hours, listening to the wind howling down the chimney, which always sounded like thousands of voices echoing eerily through the cottage. Sometimes the wind would cause the bedroom door to blow open, and I would put my head under the blankets and hold my breath, just in case my dead ancestors knew I was still awake.

Although my mother would frequently visit us in Ireland, she never really stayed very long. Although I missed her very much, I was getting quite used to her short visits, until one day she returned and told us we were going to begin a new life in London, England. Although I was very sad to leave Granny Helen, I was also excited to be going to live in England. I'd heard so much about London, and how it was the capital of England, full of opportunities and the chance for ordinary people to be successful. I wanted to be wealthy, and have enough money to buy my mother and siblings a nice big house. Then my mother wouldn't have to worry about anything. From that moment on I had already decided that this was to be a new beginning for all of us.

My gran, and my mother's three sisters, Essie, Annie and Nelly cried as they saw us onto the train. I couldn't understand why everyone was crying, when after all we were going to begin a completely new life in England. Surely, I thought to myself, they should be happy for us.

The ferry across to Holyhead involved a journey I have never forgotten to this day. I was seasick and thought I was dying. I've never experienced anything like it in all my life. It was a horrible experience, and I was so glad when the boat pulled into Holyhead and I could walk on solid ground again. Needless to say, that journey put me off the sea forever, and from that day to this I have never been on a boat and never will!

Chapter Two
A New Beginning in England

On our arrival in England we went to stay with my father's sister, May, and her husband, Len. They lived in Tollington Way in Islington, London, and although their flat was already overcrowded with their own two children, Sheila and David, they couldn't have made us more welcome. Uncle Len was an extremely kind and gentle man, and treated us just like his own children. He was a white South African, and had a funny accent. I loved Uncle Len and Aunty May, and loved living with them. We were just like one big happy family.

My first school in Islington was Saint John the Evangelist. London had been devastated by the war, and the camaraderie of the people was an example of their spirit and determination to survive together. The kids at school were a different breed to what I'd been used to back home in Ireland. Although I loved the school, I was forever being picked on because of my thick Irish accent. This seemed to make me the target for every playground bully. Even at that early age I had a temper, and wasn't going to allow anything to stop me being happy in school. I very quickly learned to defend myself, and decided that I had nothing whatsoever to lose. I seemed to always be fighting just to stop the bullies making fun of the way I spoke. Once the other kids at school realised that I wasn't going to take their bullying or making fun of my broad Irish brogue, I earned their respect and became one of them, so to speak. Although life in Ireland had been completely different, I was gradually becoming more streetwise here in England. Eventually I was fully accepted by the other kids, and although I didn't consciously try to hide my Irish accent, I gradually became more and more of a Londoner. This meant that I now fitted in, and really did feel at home. Then, the inevitable happened, and the council found us our own flat. Within weeks we moved to the new flat in Almedio Street in Tottenham. We moved with our furniture on the back of an old lorry. I'll never forget that day. I hated leaving Saint John the Evangelist and all my friends. This meant starting all over again and having to prove myself. At least now my accent was not as noticeable and I had become a lot tougher and more able to stand up for myself.

The new school wasn't so bad, and the kids here didn't seem to care about me being Irish. I was still the mischievous, inquisitive little boy, and always liked to explore places I knew I shouldn't explore. By the time I was thirteen my mother's new partner, Ron Hooker, had moved in with us. He looked after his younger brother, Allan, and so I suppose was used to kids. They do say, 'It's difficult for a man to accept another man's kids'! But, I must say, Ron Hooker did care for us, and although I never really looked upon him as my father, he did take care of us as best as he could. He seemed to make my mother happy, and that's all that mattered to me. They couldn't marry, as this would have meant that my mother would have lost dad's war pension. However, someone informed the authorities that she was living with someone and the pension was immediately stopped. This meant that they could now get married, and make the whole thing legitimate. In those days, 'Living over the brush', as it was then called, was frowned upon a little, and so being married made it just right! Anyway, at least we were a family again.

I was always getting into trouble in one way or another. I suppose you could say that I had an inquisitive nature and would always go where I wasn't supposed to go. When I think back there were some quite hilarious situations that at the time were quite frightening. Late one night a few of my mates and I decided to explore the crypt of Saint Mary's Church, in Upper Street, just to see what was in there. It was very dark and we were looking for a way into the crypt, which was down some stone steps. It was an ideal night for making ghostly sounds and scaring each other. Eventually, we found a hole in a window and the four of us crawled through, one after the other. The moonlight filtered through the grimy windows, and cast eerie shadows across the cold stone floor. Although it was quite frightening and very spooky, we loved it!

There were coffins lined up along one wall, and we heard an eerie groaning sound echoing through the crypt. We all froze to the spot, and all the hairs on the back of my neck stood on end.

9

We all swung round together to look in the direction of the noise and could see a shadowy figure sitting bolt upright on one of the coffins. We were so frightened we could not move an inch, and watched in sheer terror as the shadowy figure of a man in a long coat swung his legs over the side of the coffin and began making his way towards us, mumbling his displeasure. We all screamed in unison, and one by one made a mad dash for the window, pushing each other frantically out of the way, to avoid being the last one to escape. It wasn't until we had made our hasty retreat and were standing in the safety of the churchyard outside that we discovered that our ghostly assailant was not a ghost at all, but a tramp that had been sleeping in the crypt. We got the fright of our lives, and I swore that from then on the crypt was out of bounds, to me at least.

Some of my childhood adventures were not so funny, and were even life-threatening. When I was thirteen my mischievous curiosity led me into a stonemason's yard. I fell into a lime pit and some of it went into my right eye. The lime burnt the cornea of my eye, and caused me to lose most of the sight in it. Over the years my left eye somehow compensated for the weakness in the other eye. It never bothered me and I just got on with my life, just like every other kid during the war years. Anyway, the accident did not deter my sense of adventure, and I always enjoyed a challenge, regardless of what was involved. Even at the age of thirteen I did everything I could to help my mother and pay my way. In those days the roads used to be laid with tar blocks, and these would occasionally be renewed. I used to go to the local council yard and buy as many of the used ones as I could, and then sell these to local builders. Although my mother was ashamed of me doing it, this little enterprise certainly helped her and Ron to pay the rent. At that time Ron wasn't working, and money was very scarce. He was an engineer, and there didn't seem to be much need for engineers at that time. They were desperate for builders to help with the reconstruction of London, and Ron was just taking temporary work when and where he could. When I wasn't selling tar blocks, I used to buy large cartons of ice-creams and ride round the streets of North London on my bike, with a small cooler on the front, selling them to the kids. I most certainly had an aptitude for making money, and this prepared me for my later life. Thinking back, I must have been quite an entrepreneur even then.

I had always been a dreamer, and was frequently being shouted at by Ron for daydreaming. I used to sit there staring into space, watching faces and different shapes passing through my mind. I now know that this is quite common with psychic children. Sometimes I would see the figure of a man standing at the foot of my bed, just watching me through the darkness. Although I was never too sure, I used to think it was my father calling to see how I was. I certainly had the 'Celtic Eye', just like my Granny Helen, but I had no idea that one day I would be a practising medium, taking Spiritualist meetings and working in theatres all over the UK.

Even in spite of all the things I got up to as a child, I was still a very religious little boy, and used to pray for at least two hours every day. I did this to ensure my entry into heaven. We were also told that if we attended church for nine months, we would most certainly be guaranteed a place in heaven. Unfortunately, I could never make the nine months. I managed to attend church for eight months, but never the nine. I always hoped that my two hours of praying each day would get me there when I died anyway.

Ron and my mother always seemed to be rowing and screaming at each other, over one thing or another, and there never seemed to be any peace in the house. My mother noticed that I was beginning to develop a very bad stutter, and sometimes would seem to be quite depressed. I suppose I was feeling rather unhappy with all the rowing.

Sometime around 1947 our family relocated to 37 Toppham Street in Tottenham. It was around that time my mother gave birth to my sister, Doris. For a time she and Ron seemed to be quite happy, and the new addition to the family seemed to completely transform the atmosphere around the home. I became quite introverted and began staying in a lot. There was a heavy downpour of snow, and the road was crowded with kids throwing snowballs and building snowmen. The snow must have been six inches deep, and the traffic was almost at a standstill. Ron stood in the doorway watching me impatiently. 'Come on!' he bellowed. 'Get your coat on and go and have some fun in the street. It's not natural for a kid of your age staying in all the time.'

Before I knew it, he had pushed me through the door and into the cold. It was freezing, but I really did enjoy myself. I initially thought that Ron was being cruel to me, but when I look back I can see that he made me play in the snow for my own good.

I used to love arriving home from school. My mother would always have a warm meal ready for us. We never had a tablecloth in those days. The table would always be covered with the News of the World, and when we'd finished eating, that would be cut up into pieces and stuck on a nail in the toilet. Toilet paper too was scarce in our house, and so we had to make do with the daily newspaper.

By the time I was fifteen money too seemed to be very scarce. Ron wasn't working and there were days when we had nothing at all to eat. I decided to take matters into my own hands and go out stealing food from shops, or anything that I could sell to make some money. In fact, things got so bad that Ron used to sole and heel all the kid's shoes with the inside of old motor cycle tyres. Although neither Ron nor my mother really showed their love to us, we knew we were loved. They could have put us in the cottage homes, or just abandoned us. So, we knew they loved us. Looking back I can see that life was extremely difficult for my mother. She was always tired, and looked worn out at the end of the day. Little wonder with all that she had to contend with. Through all this my need to pray and be by myself became more and more important to me. Although I frequently had what I called 'visions', I never dreamed that I was psychic. I attributed the strange things I saw to God, and the result of the amount of praying I did. Nobody made me pray, I just felt a deep need to do so. In fact, I always felt turmoil in my heart. Even at that young age, stealing and all the other wrong things I did affected my conscience very much. But stealing was a necessary evil in those days, and I just wanted my mother to be happy. I suppose this might sound somewhat strange, but from a very early age I did feel different, and always had a strong sense that I had been born for a special reason. What that reason was I had no idea. I just knew that I was going to achieve something in my life.

Chapter Three
Becoming a Man and a Criminal

For some reason, when I was fifteen I began to have a huge chip on my shoulder. I don't know why, but I felt extremely angry with the world. I watched my mother struggling to feed the family and felt quite helpless. I began mixing with the wrong people, who showed me how easy it was to get money. This gang had made quite a lot of money robbing sub-post offices, and this somehow appealed to me. I naively believed that I could do the same and that this would solve all our family's problems. I didn't need much encouragement to accompany them on one of their jobs, but unfortunately things did not go according to plan. The robbery went completely wrong, and although I got away, one of my friends got caught and gave my name to the police so that he would receive a lighter sentence. I was sentenced to two years in a young offenders' remand home, with some of London's toughest teenagers. I knew that I would have to be tough in the place and stand up for myself. I had to clean toilets and dirty marble floors, and the bullies of the remand home were forever picking on me. Although I stood up for myself, sometimes I got the beating of my life. You had to keep your wits about you, and try to be as sharp as everyone else.

I made a few friends in that place, but I also made a few enemies. You only had to look at someone sideways, then that was it. Occasionally some of them would gang up on you. When that happened I would just put my head down and get stuck in to the toughest of the group. I hated every minute of it, and that was probably the most difficult period of my life. One of the guards tried to sexually assault me, and when I stood up to him and he saw that I wasn't having any of it, he made me get in the boxing ring with the toughest lad in the remand home. Luckily I gave him the hiding of his life, and this earned me a lot of respect. Fortunately, I'd only been there three months when my dad's sister, Aunty May, appealed against my sentence. She told the judge I could go and live with her and that she and uncle Len would take care of me. Luckily, the judge agreed and I was released into Aunty May's care.

I returned with aunty May to her home in Islington, and the place where I had previously been very happy. From then on my life changed in more ways than one. I became more and more introverted, quiet and very shy. Aunty May and uncle Len really cared for me. The fact that I liked spending time by myself seemed to heighten my sensitivity and made me more and more psychic. Sometimes I would think it was all in my mind, and that I was imagining the things I saw. The whole thing made me extremely religious, and for a while I thought seriously about becoming a priest. However, I knew that this would not be practical in that day and age, and that the times were hard and I needed to survive. If anybody suspected that I'd thought about entering the seminary to become a priest, I'd never have lived it down. And so I didn't know what I was going to do. By the early fifties there seemed to be a lot of gangs around in London. This was the 'Teddy Boy' era, and every young kid was trying to prove just how hard he was. The whole city was still recovering from the war, and as food was still rationed, there was an awful lot of black market stuff around. This meant that there was a lot of crime, and whether I liked it or not, I was involved, if only to pay my way. Although I tried to keep a low profile, it was difficult for a young lad to go straight, and the more I tried to avoid trouble, the more it seemed to come my way. I was always getting into fights; some I won, and others I didn't. I was always going home with black eyes and cut lips. In fact, if you didn't have some sort of facial damage to prove you'd been in a fight, the other lads thought you were a sissy or something. You had to prove how hard you were all the time. When I look back now I can see just how unintelligent we were in those days.

As conscription was in force then, as soon as I turned eighteen I was called up into the army. I had my medical in Russell Square and tried everything I could to fail it. But even the fact that I was partially sighted in my right eye didn't seem to interest them. I even tried using my stutter as a means of avoiding being called up. Anyway, they saw right through me and I passed the medical, and was then taken into the army. Being partially sighted in my right eye, I don't know how they expected me to fire a rifle! As it turned out I was never able to hit the target, and always seemed to fire the rifle up in the air somewhere, miles above the intended target. It was quite hilarious when I now think about it. I deserted a few times, but was always caught in a few days and thrown into the guardhouse. Eventually, I settled down and just made the most of it.

Although I was never sent overseas, I was moved around from camp to camp. For a short while my psychic abilities seemed to disappear. I am sure that this was primarily because my mind was elsewhere occupied, and in the army there was no room for mamby-pamby soldiers. There were some hard men in the army and I had to stand up for myself. And so, I suppose there was no time to be sensitive, or let the other guys see that I was different! I was eventually moved to a camp in Berkshire, where I worked on a huge supply unit, looking after food, clothes, guns and all sorts of stuff. A young lance corporal began picking on me all the time for no particular reason. On one occasion he stood right in front of me, screaming loudly, with his face pressed up to mine. As he was shouting into my face he spat on my mouth. I lost my temper and punched him in the face and knocked him out cold. I ended up on a charge and spent some time in the guardhouse. Apart from that, I did enjoy my two years in the army. We were in charge of the stores, and occasionally they would hold an auction to get rid of any surplus stuff. Blind lots would be made up, and so the dealers would not have a clue what they were buying. They used to give me a few quid to tell them what was in the different lots, and so they knew what they were bidding on. I had quite a lucrative business going with this and made an awful lot of dosh out of it.

While I was in the army I discovered that my mother had had a baby just after my father was killed during the war. Because she wasn't married to the baby's father, and to avoid the stigma, my grandmother looked after him for a while, and then later my aunty Nellie took him. These days nobody cares whether or not you're married when you have a baby, but my mum worried about things like that. She'd kept it a secret for years, and so when this guy called Anthony turned up, saying that he was our brother, I didn't want to know. I wondered what the hell was going on. At first I couldn't believe it, and I couldn't even look at the lad. Although it wasn't his fault I did feel a lot of resentment and anger towards him. My brothers and sisters were not affected by him in the same way that I was, and I couldn't understand their logic. Even when my mother died I wouldn't have anything to do with him at the funeral. I know it was selfish of me, because he must have been grieving for her too. Even today I don't have anything to do with him, if I can help it that is. I know it's hypocritical of me, but the whole idea of my mother having another son and us not knowing a thing about it made me feel angry. The funny thing is, seeing my life story written down in this way has somehow made me feel sorry for Anthony, and made me think that maybe I should get to know him. After all, he is my half-brother, and you only have one life. Or, do you? That's another thing; do we only have one life? I'm not too sure! Anyway, for a while I was really angry with my mother for keeping it from us for so long. When I think about it I'm glad that we found out about him while she was still alive. She could have taken the secret with her to the grave, but she didn't. I thank God for that at least!

Apart from all this emotional stuff, which I couldn't really handle in those days, I was quite happy in the army. I even lost my virginity during those two years in the army. A woman soldier took a fancy to me, and we used to meet up every day. She used to give me a quid or two when she got paid, and would also keep me well-supplied with Players cigarettes. One night she took me into the cemetery and had her way with me on a huge family tombstone. But when she told me she was married I decided to call it a day and give her a wide berth.

The sergeant discovered that I had all sorts of scams going on, and that I was selling butter and other items of food from the stores. Although they didn't put me on a charge, they did move me away from my post on the stores, and so my little earner came to an end. I made quite a lot of money selling stuff in this way, and so when they moved me I missed the extra cash. From then on I just kept my head down and got on with the rest of my army life.

By the time I had been demobbed from the army, I had become even more streetwise and had learned all the streetwise scams in preparation for civvy street.

When I left the army I went to live with Aunty May and Uncle Len again. My mother expected me to go and live with her and Ron, but I just couldn't forget that she had told the court that she couldn't control me. Had it not been for Aunty May speaking up to the judge for me, they would have surely kept me in the remand home. Although my mother was upset, I just couldn't forget what she had said in court.

For a while I found it quite difficult settling down to life in civvy street. I missed the camaraderie of my army mates, and didn't know what to do with myself. Aunty May bought her son David a Humber Snipe car. It was an absolutely magnificent vehicle, and gave us a bit of freedom. This meant we could get out and about and pick up some girls. David was a good-looking bloke, and the girls always fancied him. Although I thought quite a lot of him, I did feel a little intimidated by him sometimes. On one occasion we picked two girls up and took them for a drive. The one David was with preferred me and so we swapped over. He was a little bit annoyed that the nicest one of the two preferred me. He couldn't believe it, and sulked a little bit. David was a fast and careless driver and was showing off. It had been raining and the roads were wet and greasy. He failed to negotiate a sharp bend and the car skidded and crashed through some cemetery gates and ended up on its roof. Although we were badly shaken, apart from some minor cuts and bruises, we were unhurt. The accident probably looked worse than what it actually was, and so an ambulance was called. After we were checked over we were

21

discharged.

I carried on seeing Pam, which made David even more jealous. She seemed to like me a lot, and I loved being with her. We saw each other nearly every day, and then she told me she was pregnant. Nine months later she gave birth to Paul, my son. He was a beautiful baby and I was so proud to be a father. She was only nineteen and I had turned twenty, and so we were far too young to settle down. However, when a girl was pregnant in those days, the man was expected to do the honourable thing and marry her. And so, that's what I did. I proposed, and she accepted. She wanted a big white wedding, and although traditionally the bride's parents should pay for the daughter's wedding, I insisted that I should pay for the whole thing, and so I borrowed enough money to give her the wedding she wanted.

Although it was quite nice to begin with, the marital bliss soon evaporated. When I think back, I do feel so sorry for her. She put up with an awful lot with me. But, in some ways she knew what she was marrying. I never really hid anything from her, and made it clear from the very beginning that I wasn't really the kind of bloke to settle down. She said she understood me, and that she loved me and wanted to spend her whole life with me. I wasn't easy to live with, and we really didn't have an awful lot in common. Nonetheless, she gave birth to our second child, my son Ian, and for a while things seemed to be fairly happy again. We had are ups and downs like every other couple, but we seemed to be getting by. Then, one afternoon I returned home from watching Tottenham Hotspurs playing at home, and Pam complained that she had a headache and felt cold. She put on a pair of my socks to keep her feet warm, and sat huddled over the fire. She seemed slightly confused and disorientated, and then suddenly collapsed on the floor, foaming at the mouth. I didn't know what to do. I never know how to cope in situations like that at the best of times. I thought she was dying and just panicked. I fetched a neighbour to have a look at her, and she immediately called for an ambulance and Pam was rushed to hospital. I will never forget sitting in the ambulance with her and listening to the piercing sound of the bells ringing as it raced through the streets of North London. I was terrified as I watched the ambulance attendant standing over my wife as she lay there, ashen-faced and looking as though she was dead. Although we hadn't been getting on for some time, I did feel so terribly sad and afraid that she was going to die. I cried in the ambulance and just felt so helpless. I also felt a little guilty for not really being a good husband. I made a promise to myself that if she got better things would be different, I would make sure of that.

The journey to the hospital seemed to take forever, but eventually we arrived. There was a lot of commotion as they gently transferred my wife onto a trolley and rushed her into the emergency unit. They seemed to take forever examining her, and even made me wait outside the ward while they carried out all the appropriate tests. I expected them to come out at any moment and tell me she was dead. I could feel my heart racing and I couldn't breathe, and at that moment I really did feel alone. They eventually diagnosed a brain haemorrhage and said that they didn't expect her to survive the night. I didn't know what to do, and somehow felt guilty for not loving her the way I should. I sat by her bed day and night, holding her hand and quietly speaking to her, in the hope that she would wake up from the deep coma. She eventually came out of the coma after six weeks. The doctors were quite amazed, but said she would not be the same woman, and that it would probably take her at least two years to recover some semblance of normality to her mobility.

Her whole personality changed, and she seemed to become more and more aggressive towards me. On one occasion she threatened me with a knife, and I was so terrified that one day she would actually stab me to death. She'd become a completely different woman, and her unpredictable moods meant that I never knew what I was coming home to. I decided to get a job away and would only come home at the weekend. I came home one night unexpectedly, and because I'd forgotten my front door key I had to climb through the window. She seemed to be surprised to see me, and so I accused of her of being with another man. She hadn't, of course, I know that now, but I was so suspicious in those days. I went berserk and decided that I'd had enough. 'I can't live like this anymore!' I told her in no uncertain terms. 'You can leave, or I can leave, you choose.'

She decided to remain in the flat with the kids, and I left. It was difficult at first, but I had to make a new start. At least now I was free of all the aggression and uncertainty. It was destroying me and, to be fair, I am certain it was destroying Pam. I'm not sure that she ever really loved me, but when children are involved it is always difficult making that final break. I had made the decision to move on, and although I loved my two sons very much, I knew that all the rowing was doing them a lot of emotional damage. Even though I knew Pam would most probably turn them against me, for their sakes I had to make that final and all-important break. I was a very difficult man to live with, and so I really do have to take a lot of the blame. I was never really a loving husband, and I suppose I was selfish in many ways. I can't blame Pam at all, and just hoped that she would find happiness, and that my two sons would be secure and happy once all the arguing had stopped. I know everyone blamed me for the break-up, and for a time I had to put up with all the snide comments and veiled innuendoes. In fact, it took me a long time to convince those who knew us that I never laid one finger on my wife, as some people said. It took me some time to get my life back together, but eventually I did. I don't see my sons at all today, and only very occasionally speak to them on the phone. Thanks to their mother they do blame me for everything, and I only wish they knew the truth. Still, life goes on, doesn't it?

Chapter Four
Moving On

Although the break up with my wife Pam was quite acrimonious, and did a lot of emotional damage to me, it was a huge learning curve for me in more ways than one, and had a profound effect on my sensitivity. From then on I felt a great deal of emotional turbulence within, and I always seemed to be constantly fighting with myself to lead a normal life, whatever a normal life was. I became extremely fractious and always had a short fuse. I went through a short period of depression, and it was during that period that I began having some very unusual paranormal experiences. I would frequently be visited by deceased friends, particularly in the middle of the night. Images would flash through my mind, just like watching a movie on a television that I couldn't turn off. I was quite unnerved by the experience at times, and didn't know what to do. All that I knew was that I had to shake myself out of it and pull myself together.

Although I had been psychic since I was a child, I didn't have a clue what it was all about. In those days mediums were not as public as they are today, and even Spiritualist churches were not as widely known then. Because of the circles I moved in, my intuition was extremely sharp, and I could sense danger long before it came upon me. I began catching up with old friends, the villains of north London, and gradually found myself involved in all sorts of capers. I seemed to have the Midas touch in those days, and seemingly couldn't do any wrong. Everything I did made money, and the more money I had, the more friends I had around me. I can look back now and see that they were not all friends, but just hangers on. I did have some good friends who have stuck by me, and are still there today.

Before I go any further, I must make it clear that in no way was I an angel. Far from it! I was a pretty hard fellow in those days, and would seize any opportunity to make a few quid, regardless of what was involved. Although I didn't realise it at the time, I somehow gathered around me a few of my own followers. These consisted of guys I had known for many years, and also the younger element who were feeling their way, and trying to move up. As long as they were loyal to me, I really didn't mind. I suppose some of the guys around me admired me a little. I always had a woman on my arm, even though this was very often for show. I suppose I was ruggedly handsome, with a good chat-up line. I knew how to impress the ladies, and knew exactly what they liked. I always liked nice clothes, and always wore a tailor-made suit and expensive shoes. Yes, I suppose I really did look the bee's knees. At least, I thought I did. Whenever my dear mother saw me looking admiringly at myself in the mirror, she would always shake her head and say, 'Self-praise is no recommendation.' I suppose she said this because I always used to kiss the mirror, and say, 'You handsome devil!'

I hadn't seen my mother for some weeks, so I called round to see her with some flowers. When she answered the front door she was crying. 'What's the matter, mum?' I said, concerned, thinking someone had died. 'Why are you crying?'

She told me that she borrowed money from a moneylender, and because she couldn't pay him back he had doubled the interest. I was fuming. My mother was a proud woman and didn't want to ask me for money. I could feel the rage run right through my body when I thought some guy had done this to my mother. She told me where the guy lived and I went round to see him. 'I'd like to borrow some money', I said. 'Need to decorate the house.' He took my details and said that he'd bring the money to my house later that evening. I borrowed £300, and took it immediately round to my mother. The day he was due to call to my mother's house for payment I was waiting for him. When he saw me the colour drained from his face. 'What are you doing here?' he asked.

'This is my mother', I said, squaring up to him. 'I've given the money I borrowed from you to her. And if you ever come near her again I will break every bone in your body. Do you understand?' Unable to speak, he nodded his reply. 'And you can forget the money I borrowed from you. Look upon it as compensation for the grief you've caused my mother.' He nodded in agreement, turned round, and then took off down the street. He couldn't do anything else. That was the last thing my mother saw of him. She had been far too proud to ask me for money, but promised never to go to loan sharks ever again.

The Swinging Sixties really did swing for me, in more ways than one. Everything seemed to be happening, and it would seem that I couldn't put a foot wrong.

I went on to set up a few businesses, one being a scrap metal business, and the other a used-car showroom. Of course, these were not totally legitimate, and my car showroom frequently sold on cars of a suspicious nature, if you understand what I mean. Although some of the cars I bought were extremely dodgy, I didn't keep them very long and always had a buyer ready! It was a very fast and lucrative turnover, and word was quickly spreading that I was always in the market for a good deal, where motors were concerned. The Old Bill knew what I was up to and started putting the pressure on me more and more. In fact, they used to call in regularly for a sweetener, and I would always have an envelope ready for them with a few hundred quid in it. Somebody told me that the scrap yard was under surveillance, and that the Old Bill was monitoring my movements. I didn't care at the time as long as I kept on paying them, I knew they would look after me. I found out there was a particular policeman who had it in for me. I had a word with the police officers I was paying, and they warned him off me. I didn't have any trouble after that.

My scrap metal business attracted some dodgy characters, and although I made it my business to only deal with the people I knew, I was still occasionally threatened by villains from other parts of London, who wanted a piece of the action. I wasn't afraid of anything in those days. Anyway, at the time I was with a very heavy firm, consisting of some of the hardest men in the London underworld. All sorts of things passed through the scrap yard, from gold bars to platinum. As long as I was receiving my cut I never asked any questions. I was frequently given a large sum of money to crush one vehicle or another, and because this was an easy earner, I just did it, no questions asked! Anyway, sometimes it was far better not to know anything; in that way I kept a clean nose, and then the police could not pin anything on me. Besides, there was a certain code of honour amongst the gangster fraternity, and as long as you only dealt with the people you knew, everyone would look out for each other.

At one point I had so much money that I didn't know what to do with it. I even set up a building firm that also proved to be quite lucrative. It may sound difficult to believe, but I still have a conscience today about the things I used to do. I know they do say that 'A leopard can never change its spots!' But I totally disagree. I most certainly have changed, in more ways than one. However, it's funny the way you get gradually pulled into situations, often against your will! They say 'If you lie down with wolves, you will stand up with fleas'. This is quite true! But the one thing I have learned in my life is that you can very often trust more people in the criminal fraternity, more than you can in the everyday world. That's a fact. Criminals do have a lot of respect for those who respect them.

I gradually found myself mixing with some very hard and dangerous men. I accompanied one of the hardest lads in the firm to a high rise flat in the south of London. Somebody owed him a grand and he was having difficulty getting it back. 'You won't have to do anything, Lea', he said. 'Just need some moral support, know what I mean?' The guy who owed him the money lived on the fifth floor of the building. We knocked on the door, and when the lad opened it we burst in. He was alone in the flat, and said he had no money. He didn't seem to care, and really thought that was the end of the matter. He upset my friend when he told him he couldn't get blood out of stone. 'No, but I can certainly get blood out of you!' my friend retorted, grabbing the lad by the back of the neck and pulling him over to the balcony window. I watched with horror, as he pulled open the door and proceeded to push the lad over the balcony, holding onto his legs as he hung precariously over the edge, pleading with my friend not to drop him. 'Ok, I'll give you the money.' He pleaded, 'please don't let go of me!' Needless to say, we left the guy's flat with the thousand pound he owed my friend, and so that was a job well done. That's what it was like back then. You had to be hard and keep your wits about you to survive.

On another occasion one of the boys asked me to accompany him to collect some money that was owed to him from a guy in the east end of London. Unfortunately, though, this geezer wasn't as lucky. He gave a bit too much cheek to my friend, and so had his kneecaps smashed. Once again I must stress, that I was only an observer where this incident was concerned, my friend took care of it all by himself. To be quite honest, I never liked violence of any kind, and if I could avoid it I did. There were occasions when I simply had no choice, and it was either stand there and take a beating, or do something and fight back. Mostly though I would rather take the easy option and discuss matters. If this didn't work then there was nothing else for it, of course. In all those years I never carried a weapon of any kind, and it was only in extreme circumstances that I was, on occasions, forced to use something, purely in self-defence, you understand. Apart from all that, I have always believed if you can't settle an argument with either words or fists, then the argument itself is lost.

Sometime in the early sixties, a new cabaret club opened in Highbury, Islington. This was a Mecca Club, where some of the biggest singing stars of the day used to appear. Johnny Ray, Dickie Valentine, David Whitfield … just some of the big names that appeared there regularly. It was a lively and very popular venue, and the place to meet girls. I loved music and used to enjoy going there with the guys every weekend. The club had only been open a few months when various gangs tried to assert their power and take it over. I knew trouble was brewing when many strange and very hard faces began appearing there of a weekend. I was there one night having a drink with friends, when we heard the loud retort of a gun being fired three or four times in the club's foyer. During all the commotion we stayed put, and we later learned that it had been Reggie and Ronnie Kray expressing their anger because they couldn't take the club over. I knew the twins and so wouldn't have minded them taking over. However, there was too much trouble there, and there was always somebody getting hurt. It was a pity really, the police were always being called to the club because somebody had either been stabbed or shot, and so it was forced to close down.

Even when legitimate deals were done, an occasional dangerous situation would arise. I secured a few contracts with finance companies to repossess cars from people who had fallen behind with their payments. I know it's an awful job, but somebody had to do it, and so as always I seized the opportunity to earn extra cash. It was so easy! We'd just call to the house, and if the owner of the car did not pay us the arrears, we'd just take the car and put it in the compound. If the arrears were not discharged within twenty-eight days, I would buy the vehicle from the finance company. This was an easy way of making money. I received a call one day from the finance company to collect a BMW from a house in east London. When we knocked on the door a veritable giant of a man opened it. He looked every bit the villain, rugged face and broken nose. 'What do you want?' he growled. 'I'm trying to get some kip!'

I explained that we either wanted the arrears or the key. Even when I stood up straight the man towered over me. I tried desperately to appear hard, and stared him in the face.

'I'll get the keys!' he said casually, closing the door in my face.

I looked at my friend, raised my eyes heavenward, and gave a sigh of relief. Suddenly the guy appeared at the front door again, and held a shooter to my head. 'You can either leave peacefully, or your friend can phone for an ambulance. It's up to you.'

'No problem!' I stuttered nervously. 'Have a nice day!' We couldn't wait to get away. Needless to say, we bided our time and kept an eye on the vehicle, and followed it one night to the Locarno Club. Once the guy had locked it up and gone inside the club, I jumped in the car and drove it straight to the compound. Thankfully we never heard any more from the owner of the BMW, whoever he was, and I bought it from the finance company and sold it on to a businessman from Birmingham. Occasionally I would purchase cars with a suspicious history, give them a complete makeover, change their details and then sell them on. Although not legal, this was another lucrative business, but also one that attracted a lot of interest from opposing gangs. In those days I never really cared. I walked with some of the toughest men in North London, and so I could give as good as I got.

On another occasion some people approached me from the East End, asking if I would move a large quantity of gold and silver bars on for them. They knew I had the contacts and could get a good price for the stuff, and I knew they wouldn't have come to me unless they were desperate. They had all the stuff in the back of a van, and so I told them to unload it in the yard and cover it with a tarpaulin. They left and I made a few calls. I knew I wouldn't have any trouble selling the stuff on, and I was right. I sold it all to a dealer from the north, somewhere in Manchester I recall. I told the guys I sold it for that because of the nature of the gold and silver I didn't get as much for it as I had hoped. I greatly underestimated the amount, and they didn't believe a word I was saying. I paid them cash, and one of them returned within twenty minutes, burst his way into my office, pulled a shotgun from inside his coat, and said, 'Now, I'll have the rest of the dosh! Don't even think about saying no!' Needless to say, I immediately obliged and retrieved the rest of the money from the safe. I thought that was the end of the matter, until before leaving he whacked me in the face with the butt of the shotgun. I was out cold for a few minutes, but so relieved that I was still alive. From then on I thought very hard before crossing anyone. I had developed a natural instinct and knew exactly what I could get away with. I associated with some very dangerous people, who wouldn't think twice about putting a bullet through your head. The last thing I wanted was to end up in a concrete slab somewhere, or weighted down in the River Thames. To be very honest, I lived dangerously and played very hard. I really had no fear of danger and have stared down the barrel of a handgun on numerous occasions. My friend once said to me, 'Lea, you'll come unstuck one day, old son!' I would always laugh at this sort of comment, even though my friend knew me very well.

Chapter Five
Sailing Close to the Wind

When I now look back upon my life I can see that I nearly always sailed close to the wind. I always courted danger, in one way or another, and seemed to have very little fear. I didn't know it then but I was known to be a villain, and was avoided by a lot of people. I made money from anything I could and, although drugs were about in those days, that was the only thing I always refused to get involved with. As far as I was concerned, there was plenty of money to be made from other things, and so there was no need to touch drugs. I know that dealing in drugs has always been a lucrative business, but I looked upon money made from drugs as 'dirty money', and something that really wrecked people's lives. When you consider everything else I did, I know that must sound quite ridiculous. But I did have my principles, and that's just the way I felt about drugs.

In those days if the Flying Squad knew your business was a front for some sort of criminal activity, they would put the pressure on you. More often than not, they did this so you'd give them a backhander so they'd leave you alone. This was quite a common occurrence in London in those days. I'm not saying that all police were corrupt, far from it. It was just a minority, I'm sure. I suppose they saw this as the easy option. They knew they couldn't eradicate crime completely, so they demanded payment for turning a blind eye to what we did, so to speak. It didn't matter to them what we did; as long as we gave them a little sweetener, they didn't care. Occasionally, heavies from a different part of the city would try to get a piece of my action, and would threaten to do me a serious injury. But, once they realized what people I knew, they usually backed off and left me alone. I have to say that I did live an extremely dangerous life then, and I could have lost it at any time. I had no fear, and although I do say so myself, I was a fairly hard man. I wouldn't take any nonsense from anyone no matter who they were.

Although I wasn't actually a part of the Kray's firm, I was frequently in their company. They were respected as well as feared, and they were well liked by the community in which they lived. They were extremely polite to the elderly, and really did help a lot of people with their personal problems. But then, there was the other side to them – the side you just couldn't cross. If you did, you would regret it! That's just the way it was back then. I was having a drink one night with friends in the Regency Club. Ronnie and Reggie came in, and one of their people told me to leave because something serious was going down. I asked no questions and just left. Somebody was seriously hurt that night, and if it wasn't for a friend's warning in my shell-like, I would have been there in the middle of it all. Although I wasn't a close friend of the twins, I did know them quite well, and they knew me, and I also knew they would have helped me if I ever needed it.

There's an ancient Oriental precept: 'He who rides the tiger's back dare not dismount.' This is exactly how I felt walking in the circles in which I walked all those years. Getting away from it would have been very difficult, as an awful lot of the boys would have looked upon that as a sort of betrayal. They did not take kindly to anyone who just turned their back and walked away. And so I kept on going and doing the things I did. It was around this time that the twins murdered 'Jack the Hat McVities' in a flat owned by the sister-in-law of a friend of mine. Jack had a reputation for being fierce with an unpredictable temper. I knew him reasonably well and always found him to be quite pleasant. Mind you, he probably wouldn't have been pleasant if I'd have crossed him in some way. I always tried to keep a low profile in those days. That was the best thing to do, if you wanted to stay alive that is.

I can almost hear sceptics reading this book saying, 'But what about your mediumistic abilities at that time? What about your spiritual sensitivity?' And this was something that frequently caused me to fall into a deep depression. I always had a conscience, and felt that my criminal activity was wrong. I just knew nothing else. This had become a way of life for me, and although I had always been mediumistic, I just found it very difficult to pull myself away. When I was a child I so badly wanted to be a priest, and although that notion had long since been driven from my mind, I was still very much in touch with my religious and spiritual self. I could never talk to my friends about my experiences; they would have just laughed. Nonetheless, I do believe in God, and always felt that I was being guided in the working out of my destiny. I always knew that I had been born for a very special reason, and I knew that my criminal life had nothing whatsoever to do with that reason. I also knew that one day I would have the opportunity to do better things and live a more conducive life. It may sound a little silly to anyone reading this book, but whenever I was involved in anything in the slightest bit illegal, or even naughty in anyway whatsoever, I used to wonder if I was still being looked after by my guardian angels, or whether they simply turned a blind eye to what I was doing! I know it sounds quite ridiculous, and is just like asking, 'In a war which side is God on?' You do have to wonder, don't you?

One of the spiritual turning points in my life came one cold November night sometime in the mid-sixties. I was driving back alone from a club, some time around 2am. I hadn't had a lot to drink and so I was quite capable of driving. There wasn't much traffic at that time on the roads of north London, and I'd just turned the corner and was driving down Hornsey Road when I looked in the mirror. I got the fright of my life when I saw a man sitting in the back of the car grinning at me. I pushed my foot hard on the break pedal and pulled the car to a halt. I jumped out and quickly opened the back door of the car, but there was nobody there. I could feel my heart pounding heavily inside my chest, and I was shaking all over. I climbed in the car again and pulled it over to the side of the road, staring into the mirror to see if the ghostly figure was sitting there again. He wasn't there, and I had no idea who he was. I just knew that whoever he was, he was there to watch over me. Maybe it was the same ghostly figure I had frequently seen as a child. That experience frightened the hell out of me, and made me think even more. I knew that somehow I had to change, and bring to my life some semblance of peace and normality.

Occasionally I would lend money to people. Not that I was a loan shark or anything like that, but people I knew would borrow large amounts from me, and pay back with interest. A Jewish guy I knew was in a desperate situation, and needed to borrow £30,000 for a few weeks. As I knew him quite well, I lent him the cash with no security, and he gave me his word that he would pay me back within four weeks. That was the last thing I heard from him. I tried to contact him several times, and even went round to his shop, but he was always unavailable. It became obvious to me that he was avoiding me and had no intention of paying me back what he owed me. This went on for months, and I could see that desperate measures were called for. I went round to his home with a pig's head and nailed it to his front door. When this didn't work I drove a cement-mixer lorry round to his house in the early hours of the morning, and unloaded the entire load of cement onto his driveway. This was my first and last warning to him. Luckily for him he took notice, and the following morning he arrived at my place with £30,000 in cash. If I hadn't paid him a visit I more than likely would not have got my money back.

Sometimes the boot would be on the other foot, so to speak, and I would have the wool pulled over my eyes and be ripped off good style. I was once sold a lorry load of Moet Chandon Champagne for £2,000, they said for a quick sale. I decided to crack a few bottles open, only to find that it was ginger beer, and most probably used on film sets. That was the most expensive pop I'd ever drunk in my entire life! We had to laugh though, it was quite funny at the time. However, what I lost on one deal I would make up on another. That was the way it all worked. Everyone was out for what they could get in those days. I suppose that was business. Everyone wanted to make money, regardless of the consequences. Most people I knew did respect me and wouldn't intentionally cross me. Occasionally, though, I'd come down hard on one of my friends, especially when I'd found out they'd done something underhanded, or cut me out of a deal of some kind. However, I did have a pretty good idea who I could trust and who I couldn't. Even though I had always been a fairly good judge of character, there were times when my judgement let me down badly. You had to keep your wits about you at all times in those days.

It wasn't all serious in those days. There were also some very hilarious times that I will never forget. I also met some incredibly interesting people. My friend's daughter had been booked to sing at a private book-signing event with the harmonica player Larry Adler. There was a party afterwards with a specially invited guest list. Because his daughter was singing, my friend had been invited. Me being the kind of guy I was in those days, I thought I could go along and simply gatecrash. It was quite a prestigious event with caviar and Champagne, and many famous faces. As soon as I walked in the guy on the door immediately confronted me and asked for my invitation. By this time my friend was already sipping his Champagne and grinning at me from across the room. I could see Larry Adler a few feet away, signing copies of his autobiography and chatting away to his guests. I looked at the doorman and shook my head impatiently. 'I'm Mr Adler's godson.' I said, walking further into the room. I knew Larry Adler had been listening to what was going on, and he turned to face us. 'Isn't that right, Larry?' I said cheekily. He smiled, and raised his hand for them to allow me in. 'Yes, of course it is! Nice to see you, son!' I was allowed in and spent the rest of the night drinking with Larry Adler, my adopted godfather. He thought it was quite funny, and was impressed by my cheek. We met up on numerous occasions after that night, and kept in touch with each other right up until the day he died. As well as being an extremely talented man, Larry Adler was also a really nice guy, very down-to-earth and approachable. I continue to listen to his records today, and I've still got the copy of the book he signed for me on that night. I still laugh about that. From then on Larry referred to me as his 'godson'. I was always full of mischief and enjoyed a good laugh in those days. In fact, I still do. I've got a very healthy sense of humour, and very few people really understand it.

Chapter Six
In the Hands of Angels

I have always advocated that a leopard cannot in anyway change its spots! But, I have to say that even villains can have their good points. I'd like to think that I wasn't really a villain, and that I was just pulled along by circumstances. Some wise man once said, 'Circumstances shape our features, and thus make us what we are!' I do believe that, and you can quite often tell which part of the country somebody comes from simply by the way they look. I think the majority of those who live on their wits do naturally develop a sort of 'sixth sense', and I more than most have done this over the years. Even though I have led the life that I have, I have still always felt that angels were guiding me. There's no other way to describe it really, as that's exactly the way I have always felt. Even when I have been faced with some dangerous confrontation, I have always known that I would be all right, and that no harm would come to me. As I have said previously, I never thought that one day I would be working as a medium. When I was a young man mediums were always considered to be little old ladies with scarves pulled tightly around their heads, not what you see today on television, young and very theatrical. Come to think of it, nor did I ever think that one day I would be appearing alongside famous film actors in movies and on television.

I suppose many people with my background boast of having known the infamous Kray brothers, but I did know them quite well and have frequently been in their company socially. As I have previously said, they were extremely charismatic, polite and very likeable. Of course, if you crossed them in any way whatsoever, you would certainly regret doing so. I once asked them for help regarding a problem I was having with a geezer from another part of London. They told me not to worry, and I really didn't hear from the fellow again. I knew he was still alive, but he just kept away from me. And so, I'm sure either the twins or one of their people warned him off. During the early to mid-sixties, I had many near misses, where villains were concerned, and sometimes I would have to keep my head down and hide for a while until things had cooled down. To be quite honest, it was a very nerve-wracking way to live, and on more than one occasion I really did think I was having some sort of nervous breakdown.

My life completely changed when I went into a pub in north London and met my second wife, Ann, in 1972. She was serving behind the bar and I couldn't take my eyes off her. She had long dark hair and she was beautiful. If you've ever met someone and had the overwhelming feeling that you know them, even when you've never met them before, you'll know exactly what I'm talking about. I knew immediately that she was my soul mate and that she was going to be my wife. We started talking and I asked her for a date and, to my great surprise, she said yes. Until Ann there had not been anyone serious in my life. In fact, I'd always adopted the loving and leaving them policy. Ann changed all that. In a very short time I had proposed, and to my sheer delight, she said yes. I had a one and half carat diamond set into a ring I'd had especially made for her, and before I could even take it out of the box, she snatched it from me and went off to show her friends. I didn't even have a chance to put it on her finger, until later that is. We got married and I began to change and settle down. Ann was the most honest person I had ever known, and she soon put a stop to any criminal activity. She was my soul mate, and I was so happy just to stay at home with her. The only problem was, every time I heard a car pull up outside the house, or any activity in the street, I would jump nervously to my feet and peep through the curtains. 'Did you only marry me to get away from someone?' she asked, suspiciously. 'Or did you marry me because you love me?'

'Of course I love you!' I replied. 'You're my whole life.' I realised then that things had to change, and I had to move on and away from the past. I always knew it would be difficult to get away from the life I had led for the past thirty years, and I knew that if I did not want to lose Ann, I had to do it.

I really did feel that Ann had been brought in to my life for a reason. From the very first time I set eyes on her in the pub, I just knew she was the woman I wanted to spend my whole life with.

I loved her parents too. Her mother Vera was a very shrewd woman and very difficult to get to know. I think she was a bit suspicious of me at the beginning, but once she knew what I was like, we got on like a house on fire. I loved Ann's father, John, and got on really well with him. Their family name was Lennon, and I used to laugh because his name was John Lennon. He was a very modest, hard-working man. He had a butcher's shop, and I was devastated when he died at the age of eighty-two sometime in the seventies. Ann's mother was a strong woman and was in her nineties when she died in 2007. They were both lovely people and I loved them dearly. I do miss them so much.

Although there was still a little criminal activity going on around me, just enough for me to earn a pound or two, I knew that I had to start a new life, if only for Ann's sake. I wanted our marriage to work, and I had made my mind up to do anything I could to make it work.

As I have already said, I have always believed in angels and the power of prayer. To my mind, you get from life what you are prepared to put into it. If you work hard you eventually get your rewards. It's true what they say, 'Cheats never prosper!' They appear to for a short while, but they do eventually get their comeuppances. I had always felt an inner battle between what is right and what is wrong! And I suppose this was the very reason I had never been really happy, until I met Ann, that is. As a child I prayed constantly for two hours a day. I still pray today, just for a few moments when I'm by myself and feeling quite relaxed.

Sometimes I do wonder if anyone is listening, or whether I am just deluding myself. I do believe in God, but perhaps not in the same innocent way I did as a child. Occasionally I will glimpse the figure of an angelic looking woman, surrounded by a beautiful intense golden light. She seems to always appear to me when I am feeling out of sorts. When I first saw her I really did think I was dying. Although she doesn't speak to me, her very presence seems to fill me with energy and joy. I've no idea who she is, but I do have a strong feeling that she is some sort of guardian angel, who looks after me. I have never been one of those mediums who like to talk incessantly about guides and things of that nature. Nonetheless, I do know that they exist, and I'm quite sure that the lady who occasionally visits me is an angel a spirit guide, and someone who has chosen to look after and guide me during my time on this planet.

It seemed that as soon as I married Ann and settled down, my mediumistic abilities really began to kick in, so to speak. I had never really taken a lot of notice of my psychic experiences. As far as I was concerned, they were an integral part of me. However, now that my lifestyle had begun to radically change, so too did my psychic abilities. I was feeling quite confused, and it did cross my mind that I was losing it a little. It was almost as though I was beginning to see the life around me through different eyes. I never really spoke about my psychic experiences with my wife at any great length. To be quite honest I felt a little silly. I knew now that some powerful, angelic force was pushing me in a completely different direction, and I had to take control. At this point I didn't have a clue what to do, and so I just decided to grin and bear it! I know this sounds rather ridiculous, but that's all I could do. I used to seize every opportunity I could to read about the paranormal and psychic things. I needed desperately to understand what was going on inside my head. It's strange really, but there were times when I really believed I was losing my mind. Sometimes I thought I was suffering from a brain tumour or something, and that the apparitions I occasionally saw were some sort of paranoid hallucinations. Unlike today, in those days mediums were rarely heard of, and so I had no idea what to do about the things I experienced. If anyone had have told me I was a medium I would have laughed. All that I knew was that I was 'different', and that's all!

Chapter Seven
Never Go Back to Where
You've Already Been

Although the life I was then leading was fairly quiet in comparison to the one I had previously led, I still had an aptitude for making money. I had started an interior building company, and had secured a couple of very lucrative contracts. Harrods in Knightsbridge and the Japanese Embassy in London had both contracted me to decorate and maintain the interiors of their buildings. Harrods particularly was a good earner, and as the building needed to be highly maintained, there was regular work. At one point I had seventy men working for me, and although those who know me today find it difficult to believe, back in those days I was a hard taskmaster and someone who would not put up with shirkers or dishonesty.

One of the funniest things that ever happened was when I got a nice contract to regularly decorate and maintain police stations throughout north London. I was supervising the work in one of the upstairs rooms in my local police station, when I noticed some photographs of criminals on a board. 'I know that face', I said to myself, taking a closer look. 'It's my mate.' When I looked at the other photographs, mine was amongst them. There was a file of all the gangs I associated with. And there I was decorating the station. Some funny things occasionally happen. You've got to laugh!

My scrap metal business had attracted far too much trouble, and so I'd long since sold that on. Although I tried desperately to leave my criminal past behind, it would seem that my criminal past refused to leave me behind. I'd always made it a policy 'never to go back where I'd already been', and I was finding this increasingly more difficult. It wasn't that I thought of myself above my old cronies, but more the fact that spiritually speaking, something had happened to me. Of course, I would have been ridiculed if I'd have told anyone this, and so there was always this constant battle going on inside of me.

The first warning signs for me came some time during the 1970s. Ann had gone shopping, and I was sitting at the table flicking through some papers. I paused for a few moments, and then found myself staring into space, something I had done so many times as a child. I leaned forward and rested my elbows on the table, when my chair suddenly began rocking violently backwards and forwards. I have never scared easily, but I was terrified, and didn't have a clue what was happening to me. I first thought an earthquake had struck us, but when I tried to stand up, some invisible force held me down. The chair continued vibrating for what seemed like an age, before suddenly stopping. I felt exhausted and pulled myself tiredly to my feet. I was disorientated for a few moments and had to relax in the armchair. I didn't know what to make of it, and knew that nobody would believe me.

By the time my wife had returned, I had put the incident from my mind, and decided not to mention it even to her. I wasn't sure whether or not I had experienced some sort of paranormal phenomenon, or whether I had somehow imagined it all. Anyway, I just hoped the same thing would never be repeated. I didn't know it then, but I later learned that this was some sort of telekinetic energy, most probably a build-up from when I was a child, which was warning me to make a change. I did try extremely hard to make a break with the past, but I had made some very good friends over the years, and turning my back on all of them was quite difficult to do. Besides, not all my friends were involved in criminal activity, and I would have felt disloyal to those people, many of whom had been very loyal to me and given me a lot of support over the years. Anyway, I was beginning to notice all the signposts indicating clearly in which direction I was to travel.

I had always been extremely interested in antiques, and had a particular interest in fine art, and so it came as no surprise to those who knew me well when I opened a few antique shops and an auction business. I knew there was a lot of money to be made in antiques, and could already see the niche in the market for exporting to the USA. They do say that there is no room for sentiment in business and, unfortunately, I applied this precept when purchasing antiques from people desperately in need of cash. House-clearances were very often particularly lucrative, and I really did make an awful lot of money buying stuff in this way. I would like to think I had a conscience, but unfortunately I had the overwhelming need to make money, regardless of how I was able to do this.

First Out-of-Body Experience

I know only too well that tiredness can do strange things to the mind, and that extreme fatigue can even cause hallucinations. However, I have always regarded myself as fairly well grounded, and not someone who allows his imagination to run away with him. As a young boy I can recall having out-of-body experiences, but these mostly occurred whilst I was in the hypnogogic state, that is just hovering between sleep and being awake. My first real out-of-body experience took place when I had climbed into bed having not slept for seventy-two hours. By this time, although my body was extremely worn out, my mind had somehow gone beyond sleep, and although I closed my eyes, my head was still awash with the events of the last couple of days, with all sorts of images flashing through my brain. I suddenly felt a sense of buoyancy, as though I was floating slightly above my bed. I put this down to acute tiredness and thought nothing of it. I could feel my wife Ann next to me on the bed, and then there was a sort of explosion inside my head, and the next thing I knew I found myself floating about six feet above the bed, looking down at my sleeping body. I first thought that I had died and didn't know what to expect next. It wasn't an unpleasant experience, and to be perfectly honest I didn't want it to end. Although I did feel as though I could have moved about quite freely, I felt I had to keep my body in sight, and made no attempt to move away from it. I seemed to lose all sense of time, and the whole experience suddenly ended when, without any prior warning, I find myself back in my bed and feeling completely disorientated. Although it seemed as though hours had passed, when I checked the clock on the table beside my bed, the whole thing had taken place within no more than fifteen minutes.

I have since learned that time is non-existent in the Astral World, and what we think of as time there is, in reality, only experience. Since that one, I have had many other out-of-body experiences, and each one is completely different from the one before. I now know that the Astral World is quite surreal, and possesses a geography completely different from this world. Because I have an interest in art, I can see a great similarity between the Astral World and the paintings of Salvador Dali. Nothing seems to make sense there, and yet total peace persists. The Astral World seems to be quite abstract, and appears as though every point of its space is a point of self-created light, of a kind quite different from the light of the physical world. In fact, experiencing life in the Astral World is really quite frightening, simply because it produces a state of euphoria and complete at-one-ment with the universe. I know that sounds a little far-

Liam Scott

Liam's mum

Liam's dad's grave in Kohima, Burma

Liam's father and his mother

Alan, John, Doris, Val and Liam

Front row: Val (sister) Alan and Ron back
(step Dad) Ron, Liam's Mum, Doris

Liam's mum

Placido Domingo and Liam in Pallagica,
The Royal Opera House Convent Gardens

Liam (right) with brothers
John and Ronnie

Rabbi in *Silent Witness*

Liam as a priest in *National Treasure*
Starring Nicholas Cage

Royal Opera house as *father of the bride*

Some of the cast from the
Royal Opera house

Young Victoria Duke of Sussex,
starring Emily Blunt

Young Victoria Liam as the Duke of Sussex giving victoria away

On location, *Young Victoria,* Arundel Castle

Liam in *Young Victoria* Duke of Sussex

Liam in *Young Victoria* Duke of Sussex

fetched and fanciful and very sixties. Nonetheless, that's the only way I can explain it. Nowadays, my out-of-body experiences are completely spontaneous and out of my control. I never know when one is going to happen, and I can be lounging on the settee or relaxing in the armchair, even reading the newspaper, and the next thing I may find myself floating somewhere above on the ceiling.

So, there was a constant battle of conscience within me, and I never felt comfortable. In fact, I knew something was going on inside me, and although I would never have defined it as a 'spiritual transformation', that's exactly what it was. More than this though, I did not want to let Ann down. As far as I was concerned, she was the best thing that had ever happened to me and I did not want to lose her.

Eventually I came to a very important crossroads in my life, and then I knew that something had to be done. At one point I thought I was going crazy! Things were happening all around me, and I really did feel that my thoughts were not my own. Some time in the 1970s, a friend introduced me to singer/songwriter Lynsey de Paul, and she became a good friend, not in a romantic sense, but just someone I found easy to talk to. In fact, Lynsey is extremely psychic, and her life has been peppered with psychic experiences. There's something quite special about Lynsey, and just being with her you can see that she is somewhat different from other people. Perhaps this is why she is so talented; I have always felt that she is connected to some incredible source of creative consciousness. She'd probably think I was off my head if she heard me saying this, and I don't know what she'll think when she reads it. I often phone her when I'm feeling a little down, and she always seems to phone me when I need to talk to someone, almost as though she knows.

By the end of the 1970s my life had changed dramatically, and although I still made money anyway I could, for Ann's sake more than anything, I did try to keep my nose clean and go straight. I was doing quite well out of my antique businesses, and there was always a lot of money to be made exporting to America. A solicitor hired me to clear an old house in one of the more salubrious parts of London. An elderly lady had died and her solicitor had been given the job of selling her estate and effects. There was a lot of really old furniture, porcelain and other antique collectables. I bought the whole lot for a pittance and knew I would make a huge profit. One of the lads working for me called me to show me an old safe that was concealed in an ornate cabinet. As we didn't have the combination, we had a hell of time cracking it open. We eventually burned it open and I really got the shock of my life. Thousands of pounds worth of jewellery fell out onto the floor. Diamond necklaces, rings, bracelets and diamond brooches. I just couldn't believe it. It had been a legitimate purchase, and so it was legally all mine. That was a one-off, and I really did make a huge profit from it.

In 1983, my wife's mother, Vera, became quite poorly, and so Ann went to look after her in Colchester. Because of my work I remained in our house in London. Although I'm a survivor, and enjoy my own company, I'd grown accustomed to having Ann with me. We'd no idea how long she'd have to stay in Colchester, because although her mother was quite frail, she was also a strong lady, and someone who could live for many more years. At least being by myself I had the chance to explore my own spirituality. I read as much as I could, and began exploring the different techniques of meditation. In fact, I found a technique that suited me perfectly well, and it was through the use of this technique that other mental skills began to slowly develop. Although it probably sounds a bit far-fetched and fanciful, I did feel that I could influence people to do exactly what I wanted. In fact, I proved this on many occasions.

Chapter Eight
The Powers of the Mind

I realised very early on that it is all too easy to become airy-fairy when getting involved in spiritual matters. I always prided myself on the fact that I was quite sensible, and I would not allow my head to be in the clouds. I knew I had some sort of psychic ability, and I just wanted to develop it further. I had no idea at that point what I would do with it, but I just knew that from a very early age I had some sort of spiritual path to follow. I was relaxing in the lounge and had just entered a meditative state. Although in meditation I usually lost all sense of my surroundings, at this point I was still vaguely aware of where I was. I suddenly become aware of an extremely sweet fragrance, and was overwhelmed with an incredible sense of peace. Although I was surrounded by silence, I could hear the intermittent sound of a bell ringing in the distance, and some sort of chanting, rather like Buddhist monks in a monastery. I maintained this meditative state for as long as was comfortable, and then I felt compelled to force my eyes open. Although I felt slightly disorientated, and my vision was somewhat blurred, I could just about distinguish the silhouette of a diminutive eastern monastic figure, facing me and sitting cross-legged. He seemed to be totally oblivious to me, and was obviously in a state of deep meditation.

I moved my head to look around and was amazed to see that I was not in my lounge, but in a temple of some kind. The sweet fragrance I could smell was coming from a huge bowl of incense to the right of me, the smoke from which was spiralling up towards the ceiling. I noticed that the meditating monk was surrounded in a beautiful golden light, and there were other bright lights in the air around him. I seemed to lose all sense of time, and I've no idea how long this experience lasted for, but the next thing I knew I was waking from a deep sleep. I opened my eyes and could see that I was back in my lounge and feeling totally relaxed. I sat there for a few moments until I had fully recovered, and then I went to make myself a warm drink.

The whole experience was quite overwhelming, and I had no idea whatsoever what had happened to me. In fact, although it wasn't an unpleasant experience, I was a little reluctant to meditate after that. I have always been interested in the unknown, but I do like to be in control at all times. This experience took me unawares, and really did confuse me. 'What did it all mean?' I asked myself. 'What's going to happen next?'

I did not meditate for some days, and waited until the experience had faded somewhat from my mind. The next time I entered my usual meditative state, something else happened. I could hear the table in front of me vibrating fiercely, and when I opened my eyes I could see that it had in fact moved closer to me.

I'd read about telekinetic energy (the movement of objects without physical help), and I knew that this strange phenomenon was happening to me. At that point I didn't know whether some discarnate spiritual force was moving the table, or if it was some power generated by my own mind. It frightened me, I don't mind saying. I could feel my heart racing and my whole body was shaking with fear. I tried desperately to dismiss this experience from my mind, but the more I tried the more it kept coming back.

It was a few days later and I was talking to the woman in a nearby shop. As she was serving me with my usual daily paper, I noticed a glow around her whole body. I tried to clear my eyes, but it was still there. The glow was brighter around the woman's head, but was considerably duller around her chest. 'You're not feeling too well today, are you, Joan?' She looked at me rather quizzically, and then shook her head. 'Do you suffer with your heart?' I couldn't believe what I was saying, and didn't know where it was coming from. She looked at me as though she thought I'd gone crazy, and then handed me my change before turning to the next customer. To be quite honest, I felt a little embarrassed. A few days later I went into the shop, this time to be served by a younger woman. 'Where's Joan?' I inquired. 'Is she off today?'

'Joan had a heart attack and died!' came the shocking reply. 'She hadn't been well for some time.' I walked from the shop almost in a trance. I felt numb all over and wondered what on earth was happening to me. I had somehow developed the ability to access a person's energy field, or the aura, as it is known. This obviously enabled me to obtain personal data about the individual to whom the aura belonged. I found this quite frightening, and it was just like something from the pages of a science fiction story. I couldn't believe that it was actually happening to me, and I wasn't too sure that I wanted it.

After that many other strange phenomena occurred around me. I frequently saw light anomalies, or 'orbs' as they are called today, float around the room. I became quite accustomed to seeing these ghostly and very strange lights, and I soon learned to ignore them. I had no idea what they meant, and so I normally just carried on with whatever I was doing, and dismissed them completely from my mind. It was as though they had some form of intelligence, and the more I ignored them, the more they would gyrate and sometimes multiply. Sometimes the lights appeared in different colours. For example, although they were mostly balls of intense white light, sometimes there would be blue lights. I felt more comfortable when blue lights appeared around me. I don't know why, but I got the impression that these were connected to a more spiritual energy source. As the weeks went by, I discovered that the diminutive Easter Monk I had seen during my meditation was in fact a spirit guide. Although I've never found out his name, I know he somehow helps with the work I do today.

I eventually discovered that I could do things with my mind. I was able to influence people to do what I wanted them to do. I'm not talking about hypnosis, or making them do things against their will, but more a power that I had somehow harnessed. For example, there was a teenager on the tube holding a leather strap of some sort. He spent a good ten minutes swinging it in a clockwise motion. I sent him the mental command to hold it in the other hand and begin swinging it in a anti-clockwise motion. He did, and I was absolutely amazed. Thinking that this might have been coincidental, I sent him the mental command to stand and go and sit on a different seat, the seat on the other side of the carriage by the window. No sooner had I done this than he did exactly that.

After a little more experimentation, I was convinced that I had some sort of telekinetic power. I knew it would be wasted just using it to influence people to do silly things, and so I began studying the concept of mind energy, and how I could use it in a more effective way to help other people. Without realising it, I had always had this unusual ability, even as a child. In fact, I suppose you could say that I had used it in business, to help me clinch a deal, or even to seize a business opportunity. Now I wanted to develop it further. At this point in my life I still had no aspirations towards being a medium and speaking to the so-called 'dead'. However, little did I then know that this is exactly what I would be doing many years on.

Chapter Nine
A Thousand Mile Journey
Begins With a Single Step

I now fully understand what is meant by 'spiritual development'. It's not about being all pious and religious; it's about changing the way you think. To me spiritual development is about transformation, and changing your attitude towards everything – things as well as people. When you've lived the kind of life I have lived, this is extremely painful, psychologically speaking. However, I had known for some years that this transformation had to happen, and I seriously addressed this when my mother died in 1984. Although I knew she loved me, and I loved her, we'd go long periods without seeing each other. She always knew I was only a phone call away if she needed me, but as far as I had always been concerned, I had a life to live, and I knew mum was ok. They do say when your mother dies you lose your best friend. I felt as though a large part of me had gone when my mother died. This was the woman who'd brought me into the world, and the woman who had struggled to look after us all. This was a new era for me, and I knew my life was changing rapidly.

The antique business was extremely lucrative and gave me a good living. Although I had plenty of dosh I can honestly say that it didn't mean a lot to me. I liked to enjoy myself and really didn't mind spending it. I was driving a new Mercedes and wore the best clothes money could buy. I know it's a bit of a contradiction; on one hand I was endeavouring to become more spiritual, and on the other I liked the good things in life. Put it this way, my childhood notion to be a priest would most certainly not have fitted into my lifestyle then, that's for sure.

After a long illness, Ann's mother, Vera, eventually died. My wife decided to remain in Colchester, at least for a while, until her mother's estate was sorted. I continued to live alone in our semi-detached in north London, but phoned Ann nearly every day. Although I missed my wife, I really did enjoy my own company. I can honestly say, whilst she was living away from me I never so much as looked at another woman. I loved and missed my wife, and that was it as far as I was concerned. Ann was and still is my whole life, and I have always felt a spiritual as well as an emotional connection with her. I know she will smile when she reads this, and most probably won't believe me. However, it is true, and that's why I have written it, to let her and everyone know exactly how I feel about her.

There was still a constant battle going on inside me somewhere. Although I still find it very difficult to describe, it was just like the good and bad parts of me fighting each other to take control. I am quite sure that even the best of us experience this from time to time, but it was a huge problem for me. I think my traumatic childhood, and the life I had been subjected to when I was young, somehow culminated into this massive conscience. I don't really understand all this stuff. Although my real education came on the streets of London and not in the classroom, I'd still like to think I was intelligent, and always knew that there was more for me to do. I knew I had some sort of a spiritual path to walk, but first had to find it. It was obvious to me that I wasn't going to find it in the life I was then living. Making that complete break was not going to be easy. I still had to earn a crust, and I knew no other way of making a living. Besides, I enjoyed dealing in the world of antiques, and over the years had become somewhat of an art connoisseur. I had an eye for a nice piece of art, and liked to adorn the walls of my home with some tasteful pieces.

By the early 1990s Ann had still not returned. We were still married, but after living for so long in Colchester, she just could not face the hectic London life. Living away from London had made her realise just how hectic London actually was. She tried desperately to get me to come and live in Colchester, but I was a London boy and all my work was here. I used to visit her every weekend, and occasionally she would come to see me in London, and we'd go shopping in the West End, and then for something to eat afterwards. She frequently joked 'I love you, but I couldn't live with you!' Maybe she meant that, I don't know. I do know that I'm not the tidiest person in the world, and my house is a typical man's place. As long as I know where everything is, then the chaos is immaterial.

I think the catalyst where my finances were concerned came when a mate of mine landed me in it with the VAT people. I received a bill for £70,000, and to avoid being investigated further, I paid it. Although this didn't finish me, financially speaking, I knew I had to keep a low profile from then on. After that the excitement seemed to go from my business dealings; either that or my heart was just not in it. As I have already said earlier on, when the money goes so do a lot of your acquaintances. I still had some good friends, and they stood by me, even though they could see I had changed.

Whilst driving to my home in north London, I always used to pass Hornsey Road SNU Spiritualist Church, and never really gave it too much notice. I became quite intrigued with the church and wondered what went on at the meetings. Little did I then know that they conducted evenings of clairvoyance and other related subjects. I always meant to pay the church a visit but never really had the time. Then one day I was driving my car and noticed that I had red spots before my left eye. As my right eye was the one that had sustained some damage as a child, I never thought anything of it. However, it reoccurred and seemed to get worse, so I went to see my optician. He immediately sent me to Moorefield's Eye Hospital. I was devastated with the diagnosis, and even more shocked with the prognosis. 'You're going blind, Mr Scott!' The doctor said coldly. 'And unfortunately there's nothing we can do about it.' I left the hospital that day in a trance.

I couldn't believe that I was actually going to lose my sight, and felt as though my whole world had suddenly collapsed. I don't know what made me think of the Spiritualist church, but I found myself making my way there. There was a healing session on at the time, and so I sat down and waited. I had no idea what to expect, but at least there was a very calm and serene feeling in the church. It was nothing like the Catholic Church I'd gone to as a child, but there was still this incredible feeling of peace. I'd sat there for over half an hour, and eventually I was led to one of the healers, a gentleman. I felt a little nervous and very apprehensive as he told me to relax, and that nothing strange was going to happen. I explained what my problem was, and he placed one hand on top of my head, and the other on my forehead. I felt overcome with emotion, and could feel a tear running down my cheek. The whole session lasted for no longer than twenty minutes, after which a nice lady gave me a cup of tea and a biscuit. I threw some loose change in the coffers, and although I did not notice any different with my eyesight, I did leave the church that day with a feeling of peace.

Over the days that followed I noticed a great deal of improvement in my left eye. The red spots seemed to disappear completely, and so I returned to the hospital. The doctor was amazed with the condition of my eye, but did say that I would need a cornea graft later on. In the meantime, I was pleased that at least I wasn't going blind, thanks to the healer in Hornsey Road Spiritualist Church. A few weeks later I decided to attend one of the church's evenings of clairvoyance. I'd never experienced anything like it before. The medium was giving messages to selected members of the audience, and as the service was coming to an end, she came to me. 'I have your mother here.' She said softly. 'She's saying that she's proud of you, and that you have a lot of work to do for God.' That was the message. I left the church that night feeling a little despondent, and very confused. I had no intention of working for God. I thought she was referring to me wanting to be a priest as a child. I couldn't understand the medium's message. Even though I had left the church feeling quite confused, I returned the following week. In fact, I began regularly attending their services, and saw as many mediums as I could. My appetite had been whetted and I had made my mind up that this was exactly what I wanted to do. How to go about it was another matter, but I knew that this was the path I was meant to follow.

I became a member of Hornsey Spiritualist Church, and was invited to sit in a 'development circle', under the supervision of a medium called Brian Dean. He was a gentle man and a good medium, and seemed to take me under his wing. Although I had no idea what to expect in the 'circle' I attended regularly each week, and then gradually things began to happen for me. I'm not too sure how, but something remarkable happened with my psychic abilities, they become more reliably consistent. One night I kept seeing a young man by one of the women in the circle. He was about nineteen and was obviously mixed race. I described him to the woman he was standing by, and she broke down and cried. Once she had stopped crying, she told me that her son, Leon, had been murdered some years before. She had been comforted by what I had said, and I suddenly realised exactly what mediumship was all about. I felt a rush of excitement pass through me, and I felt so pleased that I had given the woman some comfort. Before I knew it, I had been invited to share the platform with another medium and give messages to a small congregation. Although I found it quite daunting, I really enjoyed it and knew that it could only get better.

The 1990s were quite eventful in many ways for me. A friend of mine had appeared as an 'extra' in numerous television productions and films, and suggested that I should get involved to make some easy money. I had always fancied myself as an actor, and so agreed to meet his agent in central London. They took me on as a client, and within weeks I was appearing in various television productions. I appeared regularly in the popular soap Eastenders, and also received many other no-dialogue parts. This was great fun, and the more walk-on parts I was given, the more confident I became. I played many different parts, ranging from doctors to rabbis, from villains to priests. A whole new world had opened to me, but in my heart I was a medium, and knew that that's what I wanted to be more than anything. Although I was quite content to serve Spiritualist churches on the local London circuit, I wanted to travel and appear in theatres all over the UK. This was the next thing I needed to achieve. I didn't know exactly how I was going to achieve it, but I knew I eventually would.

Chapter Ten
The Actor and the Medium

I suppose you could say that in a way mediums are actors, as they need to be a little theatrical in order to hold the congregation's attention. I have always liked to entertain, and have always had an ego. This too, is a prerequisite of a medium, regardless of what people think. My acting career seemed to take off, and before very long I was being invited to take Spiritualist services all over London. My no-nonsense approach to mediumship appealed to a lot of people, but not to everybody. I didn't care; I just tried to be as natural as I could. Things began to move in a different direction when I read an advert in The Psychic News for Stansted Hall, the college for Spiritualists. I scribbled down the address and phone number and booked myself in for a week. The 'Week for Mediums' consisted of workshops, lectures and demonstrations with a variety of different Spiritualist mediums. I had no idea what to expect, and so without telling anyone, not even my wife, Ann, I drove to Stansted for my week of training and enlightenment. I wanted to learn as much as I possibly could about mediumship, and was willing to listen to anyone who could pass on the knowledge to me.

Stansted Hall is a fabulous manor house set in acres of beautifully landscaped gardens and lawns. It was left in the will of farmer and writer, Arthur Findlay, for the furtherance of Spiritualism and the development and training of mediums. As I have always liked architecture and antiques, I was in awe of Stansted Hall, and mesmerised by its serenity and general ambience. There were quite a few tutors working throughout the week, and we were given a choice of which courses to attend. As I didn't know any of them, I took potluck. I felt quite comfortable with the medium, Mavis Pattilla, and liked the way she conducted her workshops. Although she was an extremely hard taskmaster, she really knew how to bring the best out of her students. Although I do feel uncomfortable amongst strangers, Mavis made me stand up and demonstrate my skills in different ways. Although I wasn't completely comfortable with everything she did, she certainly had a way about her, and her methods certainly did work for me!

It all whetted my appetite, and just being at Stansted Hall with like-minded people, made me realise just how much time I had wasted. This was not only what I wanted to do, but I now knew that it was exactly what I was meant to do. The week passed by far too quickly, and I knew that I would have to return. I met some extremely interesting people during the week, but it also made me realise that it also attracted some nutcases. By the end of the week I had spiritual indigestion, and I couldn't wait to tell everyone I knew what I had discovered. I couldn't, of course; no one would understand, particularly my friends.

I was now hungry for knowledge and wanted to learn as much as I could. Someone at the Spiritualist church told me about the SAGB, the Spiritualist Association of Great Britain at 33 Belgrave Square. I went along and Billy Roberts was conducting a one-day seminar there. When I arrived he was taking a break and signing books in the foyer. He was surrounded by women, and there seemed to be no men at all, and I thought to myself 'I wouldn't mind some of that!' He seemed to be popular, and so I bought his new book, Master Your Psychic Powers, a handbook for all those seeking to develop their psychic abilities. Although I found it quite interesting, some of the material in the book was a little beyond me. I could accept the concept of the aura, but I couldn't quite grasp the meaning of chakras and all those sorts of things.

I now felt as though I was really a part of it all. It was as though I had been initiated into some secret society and become privy to an ancient wisdom. I was on a high, and couldn't get enough of it. If my old cronies could have seen me then they would have really thought I'd lost it. At that point in my life I just didn't care what anyone thought. I was now a medium and really felt as though I knew something nobody else knew. I suppose everyone is affected that way when they first start working mediumistically. I had to keep reminding myself to keep my feet firmly placed on the ground, and not to allow it all to carry me away.

Just when I thought that things were really turning in my

favour, I had a heart attack. A heart attack is bad enough, but when you're twenty feet up a ladder, it's even worse. It was a nice sunny day, and I decided to do a bit of work to the front of the house and save a few pounds. One minute I was doing some repair work to the guttering, and the next minute I was lying in a hospital bed. I couldn't remember a thing. After having the heart attack, I'd apparently fallen from the top of the ladder onto the concrete path below. I was extremely lucky to be alive. I could have sustained serious head or spinal injuries. Luckily a neighbour saw what had happened and phoned for an ambulance. I was out cold, and when I regained consciousness I was only vaguely aware of the commotion going on around me. I didn't have a clue what had happened, until the nurse quietly explained. Even then I found it difficult to take it all in.

In the fall, I'd done some damage to my spine, and was in a great deal of pain. They gave me some pain relief and I felt quite peaceful. I thought I was hallucinating when I saw a Native American Indian standing at the foot of my bed, with his arms folded in front of him, grinning. He was there for some time, and only disappeared when the nurse came to see if I was ok. I fell into a deep sleep, and when I opened my eyes in the middle of the night, there was a man sitting beside my bed, dressed in a Victorian-style suit, and sporting a thick moustache. When he saw that I was awake, he stood up and placed his hands on my head. I fell asleep again and didn't wake up until the morning. The next thing I knew the sun was shining brightly through the window, and I could hear the birds singing outside. I'm quite sure that the Native American and the Victorian gentleman were spirit guides. I have since learned that the Victorian gentleman was a spirit doctor, and he still works with me today.

I spent some weeks in hospital, and although my injuries from the fall had been quite extensive, my recovery amazed the consultant. I had to take it easy, they said, as my heart wasn't in good shape. I'm sure the spirit doctor helped my recovery, because when I left the hospital I felt like a new man. Even today I'm not convinced that I had a heart attack. I think I missed my footing on the ladder. At least, that's what I hope happened.

I returned home seemingly with a new lease of life. I was thirsty for knowledge and wanted to do more of what I'd experienced at Stansted Hall. I took it easy for the next few weeks, and used all my time reading as much as I could.

It seems to me that when the spirit world wants you to walk a certain pathway, whoever is guiding you very often finds it necessary to strip you of the material things that they think are holding you back. I gradually lost all my money, and by the end of the 90s my businesses too had all gone. Even today I like to keep my hand in with antiques, and am frequently invited to give an after-dinner speech, usually on antiques. I enjoy talking to people, particularly about something I know well. I like fine art, and used to have quite a collection. My younger sister, Valerie, is an accomplished artist, and does extremely well, considering the world of painting is very competitive and a difficult profession from which to make a good living. Although she is primarily a landscape artist, recently she surprised me when she showed me two paintings she had done of Native American plainsmen. One of them looked remarkably like the one I'd seen at the foot of my hospital bed. Although Valerie is not really into mediums and psychics, I really feel that she is extremely spiritual, and would make an excellent psychic artist. Even though Valerie is my half-sister, I have more in common with her than any of my other siblings.

For many years now an elderly spirit lady with long white hair has visited me. She would just stand in front of me, or by the side of my bed smiling warmly at me. She usually comes to me when I am feeling a little under the weather, or perhaps depressed when things are not going my way. I always wondered who she was, and thought that she was perhaps a relative of mine from way back. Then, one day, it dawned on me and I remembered who she was!

When I was a young boy of about nine, I used to run errands for an elderly lady by the name of Mrs Pena. She lived in the tenement flat below ours, and sometimes I would sit and talk with her when I wasn't at school. She had long grey hair, and because she suffered with arthritis, she was unable to comb it herself. She would hand me her hairbrush and I would spend half an hour or so just brushing her long, grey locks. She always knew when I was unhappy, and would always say, 'Don't worry, sunshine, it'll all be different tomorrow!' The funny thing, it always was different the next day. She loved me brushing her hair, and when I'd finished she would always give me a three-penny piece, and some sweets. When I realised that it was Mrs Pena who was coming to see me, I was quite touched. It's so nice to think that she remembered me, and obviously still cared. She still visits me occasionally. She doesn't say anything – she doesn't have to. Her smile is enough! When she comes to see me now, I just say, 'Hello, Mrs Pena!' She remains with me for a while, and then disappears as quickly as she came.

Chapter Eleven
Old Habits Die Hard

I was now serving quite a lot of Spiritualist churches all over London. I really loved visiting the different churches and meeting people. No one ever serves Spiritualist churches for the money. In fact, the majority of churches pay a pittance. They give you a fee, which can be anything from £2.50 up to £10, and then there are your travelling expenses on top. Most churches cry poverty, and so I always refuse my fee and expenses, and tell them to throw it back in the coffers. I was taking the carol service, one Christmas Eve, at my own north London church. Before the service I noticed a tall well-dressed, middle-aged guy who I'd seen there on many occasions. There was something about him I didn't like, and I could tell by the way he always looked at me that he wasn't too keen on me either. I'd always tried to be polite to him, but he'd always either snubbed me, or made some rude remark. It never really bothered me, and I just got on with what I had to do in the church.

The night of the carol service I noticed that he was looking at me and sniggering to his friends. I'd had a bad day, and this was the last thing I needed. The service started and I led the congregation in prayer. After the first hymn, I noticed that he was looking at me and laughing with his friends, whoever they were. I tried my best to ignore him, but I could see that he was trying his hardest to rile me. After all, it was the Christmas Eve carol service and I had to keep my cool. As always at this time of the year, the church was full and everyone was in a festive mood. No matter how hard I tried not to look at him, my eyes kept moving in his direction, and each time I looked at him he was giggling. I don't know what came over me, and I just couldn't take it any longer. The next thing I knew I'd jumped from the rostrum and had the guy around the throat trying to throttle him. Even though most of the congregation knew me well, they probably wondered what the hell had happened to me. Some of the church committee restrained me long enough for the guy to make a hasty retreat into the toilet, where he remained until the end of the service.

When it was all over he left, and we never saw him again. There were a few complaints about me from some members of the congregation, but as it was Christmas it was all forgotten. I realised that old habits do die hard; I still had a temper and would not put up with anyone mocking me. The guy obviously thought that I wouldn't do anything just because I was in a church. He was wrong, and believe me I would do it all over again. That's just the way I am! Anyway, whenever there was any trouble in the church they always called me to sort it out. The occasional couple of drunks would wonder into the service just to have a laugh and disrupt things. 'Leave it to Lee!' they always say, 'he'll get rid of them!' And so I knew I was good for something!

79

Chapter Twelve
Light on the Distant Horizon

I'd seemingly no sooner got over one major health hurdle, than another came. I was diagnosed with prostate cancer and needed surgery urgently. It seemed to me that the more my mediumistic skills developed, the more I became aware of my own mortality. I had the operation and was then faced with a few life-changing experiences, primarily related to the operation I'd had on my prostate. Life was never going to be the same again for me, and I had to get used to it and build my life around it. As I have previously said, I have always believed in positive thinking, and have never allowed anything to get the better of me. As far as I was concerned, prostate cancer was just a minor hurdle, and one that I was determined to surmount. Nonetheless, I was so glad when the 1990s came to an end, and the distant bells welcomed in the millennium. At that moment I promised myself that I was going to live my life to the full, and that I would help as many people as I could with my mediumship. I'd also decided that I wasn't going to serve local Spiritualist churches for the rest of my life, and that I was going to travel all over the UK, and hopefully to America.

In 2001 there was an advert in the Psychic News: auditions

were being held in Liverpool for any mediums wanting to demonstrate their gifts in theatres. The strange thing was, Billy Roberts' company, Robuck Promotions, an agency to promote mediums on the theatre circuit, had placed the advert. I secured my place on the audition, and travelled 236 miles to Liverpool. The auditions were being held at Woolton Hall, on the suburbs of Liverpool. I made the journey by train, and was quite tired by the time I arrived at Lime Street station. I then got a taxi to Woolton Hall, which was about five miles from the station. Woolton Hall is a manor house set in its own grounds, situated in the picturesque village of Woolton. The hall itself was built by Robert Adam, the architect and designer of the well-known Adams Fireplace. There were about fifty mediums there from all over the UK. I felt extremely tired and very nervous. Billy Roberts looked stressed with everything that was going on, and I asked if I could go on first, explaining that I had a train to catch. Although pleasant, he was quite curt and agreed to allow me to go on second. There was a capacity audience of approximately 250 people. I felt quite clumsy and was certain I had messed everything up. However, Billy later told me that I gave some excellent messages to an old friend of his.

I must have done ok on the day, because some weeks later Billy's office contacted me to ask if I would like to appear on a few of his shows. My first stage appearance was on the Cricklade Theatre in Andover. Once again I was extremely nervous, and knew that this was not like the audition in Liverpool. This was a real show before an audience of 800 people. Apart from Billy Roberts, also on stage that night was Carl Fletcher, another medium from the north. I had to demonstrate for forty minutes, and although I can't recall the messages I gave, here is some of my demonstration as recorded by Billy Roberts.

Liam paced up and down the stage, looking down thoughtfully. 'Does anyone understand a name sounding like Fizburg?' He nervously watched the audience and waited for a response. To everyone's surprise a woman sitting in the middle of the theatre put up her hand. 'I can.' She called out. 'It's Fitzburg. That is my name.'

'Then I have your father-in-law with me', Liam continued, now more relaxed. 'He is obviously not English. I think he's German!'

'Austrian!' interjected the woman. 'Born and bred.'

'He is with Hans.'

'My husband, his son.' Added the woman, tearfully. 'He died three years ago.'

'He is saying he is glad you moved out of the old cottage. It was falling down!' The woman laughed, and then quickly wiped away a tear from her cheek.

'It was falling down.' She confirmed. 'We moved last month.'

Liam concluded the message by saying, 'He says thank you for giving the watch to Rudy! Do you understand that?'

The woman couldn't speak for a moment, and then said. 'Yes, I do.'

'Do you understand all that?'

'Yes, I do! Thank you so much.'

Liam then moved to a young woman at the very back of the theatre.

'Forgive me,' he said smiling, 'but I couldn't help noticing that you have been giggling since the show began?'

'She's nervous!' said the girl sitting next to her. 'She doesn't really believe in anything like this.'

'But you made her come, didn't you?' Liam said. 'Hoping that she would have a message from her gran?'

'Wow!' came the response. 'Yes, that's correct.'

'I know it's correct', grinned Liam. 'Because her gran is with me now. She is calling Bethany. Bethany. Who is that?'

'Me!' gasped the giggling girl, disbelievingly. 'That's my name.'

'Your grandmother loved you very much, you know that, don't you? And that's why she left you all her worldly possessions.'

'She left me her house.' Said the girl. 'And her belongings.'

'You were the only one who took the trouble to look after her. Isn't that right?'

'Yes!' she answered. 'That's correct, because I loved her.'

'Your gran is with her brother James.'

'My God!' gasped the girl, with her hand over her mouth. 'Yes, that is her brother.'

'I know!' laughed Liam. 'Now, be a good girl, stop giggling and enjoy the rest of the show.'

And so the entire forty minutes went on, with accurate

messages right to the conclusion of his demonstration.

Although I'd never seen Billy Roberts work before, I had heard quite a lot about him. He was very professional and knew how to work an audience. I wasn't too keen on the way Carl Fletcher worked, and he seemed to struggle all the way through his demonstration. I was so glad when the evening came to an end, and just hoped that Billy was pleased enough to invite me to do another show with him.

A few weeks later Billy phoned me himself. 'Would you like to appear with me at the Neptune Theatre in Liverpool?' he asked. 'It's in October.'

'That's next month?' I stuttered. 'I …'

'I'll understand if you can't do it', Billy went on. 'I know you must be busy.'

'No!' I blurted. 'I'd love to do it.' I didn't even give it a second thought. At that time I was doing a lot of film and television extra work, and it never occurred to me that I might be booked to do a job. As it happened that particular date was free, and so I made certain that a few days around that date was kept free in my diary.

The day of the Neptune Theatre gig I travelled up to Liverpool by train, and Billy Roberts and his lovely wife, Dolly met me at Lime Street Station. As they lived in Heswall, Wirral, they booked me into a nice hotel in Hoylake, and I spent the afternoon relaxing and listening to music. I was more apprehensive over the Neptune for some reason. Although Billy had always been friendly and polite, I still didn't really know him, and definitely didn't have a clue what he really thought about my mediumistic abilities. I've always known Liverpool people to be warm and friendly, but Billy told me that Liverpool audiences are a very different breed. The only experience I'd had of a Liverpool audience was that one time at Woolton Hall, when I auditioned for Billy Roberts. Surely it couldn't be as difficult as that, I thought to myself!

The Neptune Theatre used to be called Crane Hall. It is allegedly haunted by one of the previous owners, one of the Crane brothers who hanged himself somewhere in the theatre. I was completely unaware of the theatre's ghostly history, and as we arrived at the theatre an hour before the show, I decided to have a wander around. Billy and his team were doing a soundcheck on the stage, and I followed my curiosity downstairs into the green room. As I reached the bottom of the stairs I thought I saw a gentleman walking through the door and into the Green Room, and so walked in after him. I stood in the doorway and saw that the room was completely empty. I couldn't resist the temptation to walk right into the room and take a good look around. It was absolutely empty. I stood in front of a small mirror hanging on the wall, and as I glanced at it I saw the reflection of a man standing behind me. I turned round quickly but there was no one there. An icy chill went right through me, and I vacated the room and ran up the stairs, as quickly as my legs would carry me. When I explained to Billy Roberts what had happened, he told me about one of the Crane brothers hanging himself.

'Nobody will go into the green room alone!' He laughed. 'His reflection is sometimes seen in the mirror!' I don't scare easily, but I don't mind saying, that night I was terrified.

The show was even more terrifying. The theatre was full, tickets having sold out two days before the event. Billy put me on second, making me really feel like the proverbial lamb to the slaughter. I wandered onto the light-soaked stage, the glare so strong that I could scarcely see the audience. I'd forgotten to explain that my sight was quite bad. Luckily Billy could see that I was having problems with the lights, and so he got the technician to tone them down. Now that I could see the audience, I felt even more nervous. The sea of faces, hungry for messages, each one sitting in expectation. I paced the stage nervously in search of my first contact. I spoke to a young woman about her deceased father, telling her that he was with his brother Eddie. She was pleased to hear from her father, and amazed to hear that he was with her uncle who had not long passed over. Even though the first contact appeared to be reasonably accurate, I did not feel that I was at my best. I knew I had to relax and be even more spontaneous.

'I know we're in a famous seaport' I began, 'but I have a gentleman with me who came from a seafaring family.' I stopped and glanced at the sea of blank faces, knowing exactly what they were thinking. 'I can see the name Giles, and I have a feeling that this was the man's name.' I knew that the name Giles wasn't exactly a Liverpool name, but I gave it nonetheless, and waited for a response. A lady a few rows away from the stage put her hand up. 'Giles was my grandfather's name', she called out. 'My family were all in the navy. Even my mother.' There was a gasp across the audience, and this was all I needed to motivate me.

'You seem to have some very unusual names in your family,' I continued. 'Your grandfather is with his uncle Silas.'

'Yes, that's correct!' she said, and pointed out that Silas was her grandfather's uncle. 'I've been doing the genealogy of the family. I know most of the names in my family.' And so the contact went on. My forty minutes on the stage passed by ever so quickly, and even if I do say so myself, it seemed to be an excellent demonstration. At least, Billy Roberts was pleased, and even complimented me in front of the audience.

After the show Billy signed copies of his book in the bar, and I chatted to some of the people. We had a few drinks before we headed back to Billy and Dolly's house on the Wirral. At that time they were renting an old farmhouse in Heswall, whilst their own house was being refurbished. This was a strange place, situated overlooking the picturesque Dee Estuary. There had apparently been a dwelling on the site since the twelfth century, and the people who owned the farm were the ancestors of the original farmers. Before I left for my hotel, Dolly made some supper, and then I wandered outside to have a look around. There was a cobbled yard outside, which led to the original sandstone farmhouse approximately twenty-five feet away. Everywhere was in darkness, and apart from a crescent moon hanging precariously over the tall chimney of the adjacent farmhouse, it was pitch black.

As I stood alone on the cobbles outside, only vaguely aware of the clatter of dishes being moved in the house behind me, I noticed some shadowy forms under the dim light of the moon, moving eerily across the surface of the ground to my right. They seemed to come from the Estuary, and then disappeared ahead into the darkness. Before I left for my hotel, I explained to Billy exactly what I had seen. 'Oh, yes', he said, in his usual matter-of-fact way, 'they're the ghostly monks walking from their boat in the Estuary'. His explanation sent a shiver down my spine, and I couldn't wait for the taxi to come and take me to the hotel.

Chapter Thirteen
The Universe Smiles at Me

I've never really thought of myself as having a morbid outlook on life, but as the years draw in I do find myself increasingly more and more despondent, and now frequently look at my own mortality. I think the primary reason for this is that my life has never really been so good, and I just wish all the opportunities that come to me today were given to me twenty or even ten years ago. In fact, life has never really been as exciting for me, and my work as a medium has opened up a whole new horizon of possibilities. Even in my younger, and much wilder years, I looked philosophically at life. I have always known that there is a reason for everything that happens, and even when catastrophe strikes, there is a deeper, perhaps a more subtle reason behind it. I am a great believer in the Great Law of Karma, or the Law of Cause and Effect, and certainly believe that everything we do produces an effect upon those with whom we come in to contact. Although now a cliché, 'What goes around, certainly comes around', and I fully expect that the universe will punish and reward me for everything I have done in my life.

During my acting career I have met some interesting and incredibly nice people. Recently I was give one of my few speaking parts in a film epic entitled *The Young Victoria*, the story of the younger years of Queen Victoria. The actress Emily Blunt played Victoria, and I played her favourite uncle, the Duke of Essex. She was very nice and so kind to me during the making of the film. A few weeks after we'd finished filming I bought two Victorian sovereigns, one for the producer of the film, and the other for Emily Blunt. A couple of weeks after that I received a silver tankard from the film company, inscribed 'from The Young Victoria'. I thought it was a nice gesture, and I was really touched. In fact, Emily Blunt was one of the nicest people I have been fortunate to work with. She was polite, extremely kind, and very friendly. In fact, during my film career I get to meet, and sometimes wine and dine, with some interesting and quite famous people. I've lost count of the times I have appeared in the popular soap Eastenders. I've got to know all the cast, and when I'm in it I'm either seen in the Vic having a drink, or tending one of the market stalls. Even though there's an awful lot of waiting around, it's great fun. I knew Barbara Windsor long before she appeared in Eastenders, and have had a drink socially with her on numerous occasions. It's a known fact that she was friends with the Kray brothers, and a very good friend of Laurie O'Leary.

More recently I appeared in the crime series, 'Trial and Retribution', and I'm frequently given walk on parts in films. As an extra I've worked alongside Russell Crow, Mel Gibson, Richard Gere and even Sharon Stone. Whilst the majority of so-called superstars are very nice people, occasionally you encounter one that won't even pass you the time of day. I always give these a wide birth, and just get on with my job. The nicest actor I have ever worked with was Woody Allen, with whom I played a priest. He was so funny and very eccentric. He was always very polite and always took the time to say hello. I have also appeared in the television series 'Murphy's Law', and have taken part in many, many historical epics. I love it when I have to dress up in period costume. This gives me the opportunity to escape from myself, and to become someone completely different. Although there's not a lot of money doing extra work, it does give me the opportunity to meet famous people. However, these days my agent seems to be getting me more and more speaking parts, so who knows where this will all take me.

As I have already established, I believe totally in the power of thought. I have always endeavoured to use the power of my mind to get exactly what I want, but it is only over the past ten years that I've really and truly come to understand the mechanics of the mind in relation to the universe. I always request the things I want from the universe. I do believe that you have to send out positive affirmations in order to achieve the things you want. I also believe that it is possible to learn whilst you are asleep. This is called 'hypnopaedia', the process of feeding the mind whilst the body is asleep. I sleep with a flat pillow speaker inside my pillowcase, connected to a cassette player with a loop system, feeding my subconscious mind with information whilst I sleep. When we are asleep the mind is far more receptive, and it is in fact possible to absorb the contents of a whole book through the process of hypnopaedia. It has helped me immensely over the years, and although I still occasionally get depressed, I know that I am far more positive today than perhaps I was ten years ago. Nothing really gets to me anymore, life is far too short.

Sometime in 2001, Billy Roberts invited me to guest on the television show he was presenting for BBC1, called 'Secrets of the Paranormal'. The first time I appeared was to talk about the paranormal and to answer questions put to me by the studio audience. The second time Billy asked me to demonstrate my mediumistic skills to an audience of around twenty people. Although I was extremely nervous, the response after the programme was incredible. The television station's switchboard went crazy with viewers asking for my phone number. This just proves how much power there is when a medium appears on television.

Around the same year, Billy asked me to accompany him to a few haunted locations in the northwest. Although I've done this sort of thing before, it's not something that really interests me. I only did it to help Billy with a programme he was working on at the time. I've always been very open-minded about these things, but I agree with Billy Roberts, that when a person is told that they are visiting a so-called 'haunted' location, then the mind takes over and creates its own ghosts and demons, long before reaching the alleged haunted place. However, on this occasion Billy did not give me any information about the history of the place we were driving to. As it turned out it wasn't a house, but an area. He took me to a place called Dawpool, Wirral, not far from where he lives in Lower Heswall. I was overcome with a strange feeling of disorientation. I couldn't explain it really, and I just continued to follow Billy as he wandered slowly around. The entire area is apparently steeped in history, with a strong Viking connection. Although I didn't know it then, there is also another macabre side to it.

I wandered off by myself and made my way past the ancient church. I stood for a few moments staring at an old house set back from the road. I felt a shiver pass through my body as I approached its high ornate gates, which prevented intruders entering from the adjacent road. I just knew the house had some sort of paranormal history. Even without going inside it, I was conscious of several different discarnate entities. I explained what I was feeling to Billy, and he confirmed that the house was allegedly haunted. A child had been murdered there, and the lady who committed the dastardly deed is also believed to roam the corridors of the house. Even as a child I was sensitive to atmosphere, and always knew when something was amiss. As I've got older this sensitivity seems to have become more acute, and I always look upon it as a sort of neurological radar system. It comes in quite handy sometimes, particularly when endeavouring to make a detailed analysis of the history of a particular location. On a more practical note, it helps me to detect when danger is approaching long before it does.

Chapter Fourteen
From Rags to Riches,
Riches to Rags

My life always reminds me of the David Whitfield song, 'From Rags to Riches', because that's exactly how it has been. Although my riches have gone, I seem to have acquired another wealth – a wealth of the spirit. It's only over the past ten years or so that I have been overwhelmed with a feeling that I have been here many times before, and that this is not my final sojourn in this world. Although I have made many, many acquaintances during my life, there is perhaps a small minority that I can now truly call 'friends'. Terry Murphy has been an exceptionally good and loyal friend over the years. During the 1950s, Terry was a flyweight boxer but takes it easy these days. He's a strong character both physically and in personality, and when he calls to see me we sit for hours and reminisce over a bottle of champagne or two. Another good friend is Cliff Tarrone. He runs the North London Auction House, where I help out in an advisory capacity. Although they are good and loyal friends, they really don't understand about the other mediumistic side of my life. I don't talk about it to them, because they just laugh. My other good friend is singer/songwriter, Lynsey de Paul. She is extremely psychic and really and truly believes that she has been guided by angels all of her life. Although I have always known this, I do believe I am guided more today than perhaps I was twenty or thirty years ago.

Private Readings are Full of Surprises

Although these days I do very few private readings, sometimes I am approached by someone I feel really needs one. One particular woman in her late twenties came for a consultation last year. She was very well spoken and seemed to be well to do, although I must say sometimes looks can be deceiving. I was half-way through the reading and finding it quite hard going. I couldn't help wondering why she had come in the first place, as she couldn't accept anything I was giving her. 'I've got your mother here!' I said. She shook her head. 'My mother's still very much alive!' she grinned, with a look of achievement. 'At least she was the last time I saw her, about an hour ago.'

I could feel my heart miss several beats, and I immediately felt like terminating the reading. 'Her name is Margaret!' I persevered, 'She is with Sally.'

The young woman shook her head and sighed impatiently. 'My mother's name is Lucy. Don't know anybody called Margaret or Sally.'

Although I never like to admit defeat, I sat back tiredly. 'I think we should terminate this meeting' I said, almost apologetically. 'I can see I'm getting nowhere with you.'

'I'm sorry!' said the woman. 'Am I difficult to read?'

I looked at her with raised brows, and then sighed my answer. She seemed to be quite pleased that nothing had been right, and she rose from the chair, fumbling in her handbag. 'I must pay you for your time.'

I raised my hand to stop her. 'I wouldn't hear of it!' I said. 'I couldn't possibly take money from you.'

As I led the young woman to the front door, I suddenly blurted. 'Margaret said you lived in Bournemouth until you were three years old.'

Again she shook her head and smiled, embarrassed. 'No, I'm sorry. I've lived in London all my life.' She shook my hand and walked through the door. I felt drained, and although it was only late afternoon, I was badly in need of a glass of wine.

I had put the incident completely out of my mind, until three days later I received a phone call from the young woman. 'I just had to phone, Mr Scott', she stuttered down the phone. 'I've just discovered something quite remarkable, and to be honest it's come as a shock!'

'What is it?' I asked, thinking that this was her way of apologising to me.

'I came to you because my father died last month, and my mother has been so distraught. I didn't know where to turn, until someone recommended you. My mother was waiting to hear what you had told me, and when I explained what had happened

96

she went ashen and was very quiet. She then broke the news to me that Margaret was my real mother's name, and that Sally was her sister. We lived in Bournemouth, just as you had said, but when my biological mother died I came to live here in London with the lady I've always known as my mother. Margaret was my mother's best friend.'

The phone fell silent, and I didn't know what to say. I certainly felt very relieved, and was the first to break the silence. 'You're adopted then?' I asked.

'No!' She swallowed to hide her sadness. 'I wasn't even adopted. This has come as a huge blow to me, it really has. Had it not been for the reading I had with you I'd never have known.'

The young woman asked if she could come and see me again, and I declined. 'Leave it for a while', I suggested. 'Come and see me in a few months time.'

She did come to see me again, and even more revelations came through during her reading. I was quite pleased, and believe me so was the young woman. I knew the spirit world would not have let me down, I just knew it. It's very rarely wrong!

Helping the Old Bill with their Enquiries

As one would expect with someone with such a colourful past as mine, I have helped the police with their enquiries on numerous occasions. However, I was consulted off the record (as it always is with psychics) to see if I could throw any light on the whereabouts of a missing teenager, Angus McDermott, who had walked out of his family home in Middlesex and was never seen again. Incidentally, I have changed his name for obvious reasons. As far as the teenager's family was concerned he had no worries, and appeared, to all intents and purposes, extremely happy. In fact, he had everything to live for and had even planned to travel the world. The policeman in question took me to meet Angus' parents, and they allowed me to look at his room and even handle some of his possessions. Although I have used psychometry on many occasions, it was never really my forte. However, on this occasion I held a small Buddha in my hands and was completely overwhelmed with the sense of the name 'Jane'. I looked at the boy's mother's anxious and very distraught face. 'Who is Jane?' I asked. 'Was this Buddha given to him by someone called Jane?'

'That's correct!' said his mother with delight. 'Jane's his girlfriend. She went to work in France and met someone else.'

'I have to tell you that your son is very much alive.'

Whilst the woman's face lit up with delight, her husband just huffed his displeasure and turned disdainfully away from me, shaking his head and mumbling. The policeman made his excuses and we left the house. He could see that there was an atmosphere, and he explained that the husband was not in agreement about me being consulted.

I told him that I felt that the lad had rowed constantly with his father, and that he had left for France. Not another word was said. Three weeks later I was contacted by the policeman who informed that young Angus had returned home, and that everything I had said had been correct. There was a happy ending to the story. Angus returned with his girlfriend, and as far as I know, he now lives with her in the East End of London, and they are expecting their first child. Although the police never officially acknowledged my help, I did receive a letter of thanks from the police office who enlisted my help in the first place. 'This is completely off the record, you understand.' The letter read. 'But your help was invaluable!'

Helping an Aged Gangster to be Forgiven

Another time a bloke in his late seventies came to me for a reading. He didn't look like the usual type of person who consulted mediums, and I could see that he'd had quite an interesting life. Although he had obviously given a false name when making the appointment, I knew his face from somewhere. He didn't have a clue who I was, but I remembered that he was a member of the twins' infamous firm. In the old days I'd seen him around quite a lot, particularly in the Regency Club and the Blind Beggar Pub, one of our old haunts. I remembered he was an extremely aggressive and very heavy person in the sixties, and didn't like anyone even looking sideways at him. In fact, if anyone so much as glanced at him for a second he would show his aggression. He was a nasty piece of work, and even though he was now much older, he still made me nervous. I wondered how I was going to relax enough to give him a reading, and I just hoped he wouldn't recognise me. It took me some time to get into the reading, and for a few minutes I just waffled clumsily until he had relaxed with me. I did everything I could to get him to open up to me just a little, but he wasn't having any of it. He'd obviously been told never to give any information to the medium. He just glared at me stony-faced, with dead and very cold eyes.

Then, all of a sudden somebody from the spirit world came close. It was man with a thick, smoker's voice. The guy sounded quite old with a broad London accent, and I got the impression it was his father. He told me that he had died with emphysema, and that he was sorry for the way he had treated his son. When I passed this information on to him, he shook his head angrily. 'I want nothing whatsoever to do with him. He was a bastard to me when I was a kid, and I hope he rots in hell!' I didn't know what to say, and I was quite pleased when the communicator withdrew.

'Look, my friend', he said, sitting back in his chair, 'I've come for one reason, and one reason only. If you're the genuine article you'll know that!'

I could feel my whole body shaking nervously, and I rested my elbows on the arms of the chair. Before I could speak I heard another voice inside my head. This time it was an angry voice, and the voice of an extremely determined spirit communicator. 'This cunt ended my life!' the voice blurted. 'I want him to know that there's no escape for him! All routes of escape are barred! It won't be long before he joins me and I'll be waiting for him with Bino! Just mention Bino, that's all!'

I looked at the guy's lined and weather-beaten face, and

somehow felt a sudden surge of confidence. 'Someone's saying Bino. That's all I can hear – Bino!'

The colour suddenly drained from his face and he sat forward. 'What's he saying?' he blurted. 'What is he saying? Tell him it was all a big mistake. I was forced into it!'

My eyes locked on his for what seemed like an eternity, and now I no longer felt intimidated by this pitiful, aged man sitting in front of me. 'I really don't think he is interested in what you've got to say.' I paused. There seemed to be some fierce dialogue taking place somewhere at the back of my mind, and the spirit voice suddenly focused his attention on me. 'Just tell him the roof is falling in, and the pipes have leaked all over the place!'

I passed this on and he lowered his head to his chest. He slowly raised his head and looked at me. 'The guy was always a loser!' He snarled, shaking his head. 'Tell him I don't give a damn! And that he can go to hell for all I care. He's probably there already.'

I didn't have a clue what any of it meant, and I discreetly glanced at the clock. 'I'm afraid that's all I can give you.' I stood up and watched as he pulled himself gingerly to his feet, gasping for breath as he did. He walked to the door, and I was sure he was going to leave without paying me. To be honest I just didn't care. He stopped and retrieved his wallet from his inside jacket pocket. '£30 isn't it?' he said, peeling three £10 notes from his wallet. In actual fact it was £35, but I didn't mind, I just wanted him to go. I took the money and he left.

This is the only problem with private consultations, you can't really pick and choose who comes to see you, and you never know who's coming into your home until they actually walk through your front door. I must say that I don't do private readings for the money, but more for the challenge and experience. I do believe that private consultations help to cultivate a more accurate way of working, and also help with the development of confidence.

Chapter Fifteen
Philosophically Reviewing
My Life

When I look back to when I was a young man, I never thought for one moment that one day I would be a professional medium, travelling all over the world. Nor did I think that at the age of seventy-two I would receive offers from major television production companies to take part in pilots for new television programmes about mediums. It's not something that has ever appealed to me. It's daunting enough standing on stage in front of 2,000 people, let alone demonstrating my mediumistic skills on television, before millions of people. Over the last twelve months doors seemed to have opened for me, at least where my mediumistic skills are concerned. I find it very surreal to think that all these opportunities have come to me so late in life, and that now the power of the universe is pushing me in the direction I never thought I would head in. However, this is exactly what has happened. I will be appearing alongside Billy Roberts and Ciaran O'Keeffe in theatre shows to promote their book, *The Great Paranormal Clash*, and this is expected to go to Broadway in New York, sometime in 2009. I've always welcomed a challenge, and this will probably be one of the biggest challenges of my mediumistic career. They do say it is never too late to start something new, and I totally agree with that.

Over the last twelve months I have suddenly begun to review my life, and realise that I do have a lot of regrets. I have already said that I do not see my sons, and that I only speak occasionally on the phone to them. I do wish we were closer, and that they felt a need to get to know me more. I'm fairly close to all my siblings, but occasionally do feel quite sad that so many years have gone by, and they don't really understand about my mediumistic abilities and that side of my life. I suppose it's the same with my closest friends. It was said somewhere in the bible, 'A prophet is without honour in his own country!' How true this is. Earlier on in the book I said that dressing up in period costume gave me the opportunity to get away from myself and become someone else. I suppose my mediumistic work does that. When I'm passing on messages to selected members of a theatre or Spiritualist church congregations, I feel as though I am not me, and that I'm actually somebody else. I don't know whether other mediums feel this way, but when I am working, my mind – or consciousness – whatever you choose to call it, is transported to another place.

When my mediumship is working well, I certainly feel a strong sense of responsibility to those to whom messages are given. For the short time that I am working I do try to put my heart and soul into the demonstration, and when it's all over, I feel on a high and find it very difficult to come down, so to speak. I'm sure that this must have something to do with the amount of adrenalin used during a mediumistic demonstration.

One of the things I have learned over the years about working as a medium is that the majority of those who consult mediums most certainly misunderstand what exactly is involved in the whole process of mediumship. For one thing, it doesn't matter how well known or how good the medium is, he or she does not have the power to call people back. A mediumistic demonstration is totally experimental, and the medium does not know what is going to happen either during a private consultation or in a mediumistic demonstration. The misconceptions people have about mediums and the way they work is what causes disappointment, and not just the high expectations when consulting a medium.

The Way I Receive My Information

When a spirit comes close to me I tend to 'feel' his or her presence, long before I see or hear them. I am clairvoyant, clairsentient and clairaudient, and have been since I was a child. Although the three psychic skills work independently of each other, they do sometimes function simultaneously. When I'm actually 'seeing' clairvoyantly, it's mostly an image inside my head, although I do occasionally 'see' the spirit person as a solid and tangible flesh and blood individual. When I hear a spirit voice it is like a sequence of extraneous thoughts passing quickly through my brain, and not really like a voice at all. Even when

I'm only 'sensing' a spirit presence, I am still able to glean an incredible amount of information. I can very often tell how the person died, where they lived, and even how they looked, just by using the psychic skill of clairsentience. I always describe clairsentience as a sort of mental radar device. Although the majority of people use clairsentience in their everyday lives, in a medium this skill is more acutely accurate. Occasionally when I'm standing in a crowded place, such as a shop or even a theatre, I am suddenly overwhelmed with feelings about someone standing next to me. This makes me feel quite uncomfortable, and although I can usually shake it off, it does have a psychological effect on me and leaves me quite drained. I like to be in control of my mediumship at all times, and although I can usually turn it on and off, there are times when psychic impulses get through the radar, so to speak. Apart from those isolated occasions, I generally cope. I am quite certain now that my mediumistic skills would not go away if I didn't want to use them anymore. They have become an integral part of my life, and if they were to be taken away from me, I'm sure I would miss them as much as I'd miss my eyes or even my legs, if they were taken from me.

One of my major faults, I think, is that I am very critical of some mediums and the way they work. I am quite certain that not all mediums are genuine, and many charlatans find this profession an easy way of making money. Although the majority of people who have a healthy interest in mediums do have a discerning eye, and so therefore know who is genuine and who is not, there are some so-called mediums that slip the net, so to speak, and even go on to achieve great heights of fame. Although for obvious legal reasons, I would not dare to mention any names, I know of one individual who has done well and appears frequently on television. I can usually tell just by looking at a medium whether he or she is genuine or not, and the person in question is most definitely not a genuine medium. I know most people will think that this statement is just sour grapes, and that I am only saying this because I am jealous. This is a fair comment, but those who know me also know that I am neither vindictive nor jealous, especially where other mediums are concerned. I have always considered myself to be professional in everything I do, and would never decry another medium in whom I truly believed. However, this particular person always appears to survive criticism and negative publicity, and regardless of what is said about him, success always seems to come his way. In fact, he even survived an exposé on a popular television programme, and today is still a popular personality on many programmes. It was once said: 'You can fool some of the people some of the time, but you can't fool all of the people all of the time.' This does not appear to be the case with this particular so-called 'celebrity' medium. And I do wonder how he gets away with it. The mind does boggle!

Although I do meditate for at least half an hour, more if possible, every day, another effective way I have for relaxing and 'turning off' after a stressful day is listening to jazz music. I love jazz, modern jazz mainly, and have a large collection of records. I have been playing the saxophone for some years now. This also helps me to unwind after a long day. I was playing it one night, and when I stopped I could hear the sound of a flute echoing through the house, even though there was nobody else there. It was quite eerie and spooked me a little. Over the years I have met most of the great jazz musicians, such as Dizzy Gillespie, Joe Pass, the jazz guitarist, Count Basie, Dave Brubeck, to name but a few. I've even had a drink with Frank Sinatra back in the sixties, and I knew jazz singer, George Melley very well. I also knew Dizzy Gillespie very well, and I've socialised with him on the odd occasion. But my favourite of all jazz musicians is Paul Desmond, the saxophonist. He is incredible, and I've got everything he has ever recorded.

An excellent jazz musician, and also one of my oldest friends, Tony Cromby, was appearing on the London palladium on a show called 'Sunday Night at the London Palladium', televised every Sunday night at 8pm in the late fifties and sixties. After the show he introduced me to Sammy Davis Junior who was also appearing on the show. We got talking, and Sammy Davis asked me where all the action was in London. We took him to a nightclub that was owned by an old friend of mine. Sammy Davis Junior was quite a character and could drink and smoke for America! We kept in touch, and we met up every time he came to London. He was a great guy with an eye for the ladies. In fact, it was through Sammy Davis that I was fortunate enough to meet another great crooner, and one of the so-called 'Rat Pack', Dean Martin. I'd always admired him as well, and loved him when he was a part of a film duo with Jerry Lewis. As far as I was concerned, they were the good old days, when music was really music. When I listen to this sort of music I become nostalgic and very depressed. It just takes me back a little.

I also have a passion for fine art, particularly French Impressionism, and am frequently employed in an advisory capacity. Although I wouldn't consider myself to be an 'expert', I do have an eye for the right piece of art, and can tell a fake a mile off. A few years ago I acquired a collection of antiques pieces, amongst which was an Asian pastel painting of an Indian god. It was a beautiful piece by an Indian artist called Jamini Roy. Nobody had heard of him, but somewhere at the back of my mind I could recall seeing his name somewhere. I put it into Christy's and they put a reserve on it of £4,000, but it actually sold for £12,000. A millionaire in Dubai bought it. As you can imagine I was so pleased, and didn't care where the buyer came from!

Chapter Sixteen
Spiritual Development and Me

I know they say that hindsight is a wonderful thing, but if only I could have my life all over again …

I know it's become somewhat of a cliché, but had I been given another chance, I have to say that I would have done things so differently. I believe that we are born with inherent abilities, and that a supreme power observes to see what exactly we make of them. However, in the majority of people's lives circumstances prevail, and the opportunity to gratify these abilities never arises. I am sure we are spiritually and emotionally programmed by the parents we are born to, and as we grow into adults the onus is then transferred to us to make what we can of the life we have been given. Some people find it very difficult to break away from the psychological hold their parents have over them. The very process of 'breaking away' involves reprogramming the mind and learning to 'think' for ourselves. The universe is never wrong, and when we acknowledge this it will always give us exactly what we want.

For the majority of people there is always a constant struggle between the spiritual and the physical natures, and although very few realise what this subtle process actually is, struggle is relentless nonetheless. Once an understanding is grasped of exactly what is involved in spiritual development, the pain of it diminishes somewhat. However, regardless of what the majority may think, the process of spiritual development is never-ending, and you very often lose what you think you have attained.

I do like to meditate every day, and do believe that meditation is the highest form of prayer, and the tool with which all great minds seek to attain the highest point of light. In fact, if nothing else, meditation helps to focus the attention and aids the cultivation of patience and discipline. Meditation has certainly helped to change my attitude towards life, and has definitely calmed me down. It might sound almost a bit of a cliché, but meditation brings out the very best in me. I don't sit in a development circle these days, but I do make a point of sitting by myself for half an hour before I retire at night.

Spiritual development is about initiating a change of attitude to everything that life entails. It's funny, but as soon as I started to acknowledge my mediumistic skills, my life began to change. I do believe that when you change your attitude towards things and other people, then things and other people most certainly change their attitude towards you. We are the architects of our own destinies through the way we think. Only the universe is right, and when we acknowledge this, then the universe will take care of us. This is a spiritual fact, and only by understanding the principles upon which our very lives are based, can we ever be free from the shackles of ignorance. I said previously that our parents programme us, and that as we grow up we should use every endeavour to think our own thoughts. Only then can we ever hope to reprogramme our minds. Our souls take care of themselves and constantly guide us with every step that we take. There are occasions when circumstances pull us down and we feel as though God has deserted us. This is truly the nature of the evolution of the soul, and the onus is on us to be vigilant at all times, and watch for the signposts that appear along our path. In Yoga this is sometimes referred to as the 'Path of Attainment', and this is a spiritual process that very often requires that you leave things and people behind.

My Tips for Meditation

To meditate it is important for you to create a 'sacred space', either in a quiet corner of your home, or somewhere in the garden. You must ensure that your sacred space is only used for meditation, and so it must be made to look like a 'special' place. It's sometimes a good idea to place some crystal pieces strategically around your meditation corner, making sure that nobody can invade it. Psychologically programme your sacred space so that you know that you can retreat there when the stress levels are high, or even when you need to elevate your thoughts. Although everyone's idea of meditation is different, meditation is simply a process of 'turning off', so to speak, giving the mind time to recuperate. Always begin and conclude your meditation with some slow and rhythmic breathing. As well as opening and closing the centres, the process of rhythmic breathing relaxes and prepares the mind for meditation.

Before you actually enter a meditative state, mentally ask yourself why you are meditating. Should you be meditating simply because it's fashionable, then you will defeat the object of the exercise. As well as affecting you spiritually, meditation has a profound psychological effect on you, and whether or not you are seeking to be 'psychic', meditation makes that all important connection between yourself and your soul.

Step One:

Sit quietly for a few moments, making quite sure that your spine is straight, and your shoulders are thrown slightly back.

Step Two:

Begin your slow, rhythmic breathing, making sure that the inhalations and exhalations are evenly spaced.

Step Three:

Once you feel quite relaxed, be conscious of the space above your head and focus your attention on your head. Spend a few moments contemplating the sky above, making it blue and very clear.

Step Four:

Slowly move your attention from the space above your head to the ground beneath your feet. Feel the weight of your body on the chair, and then the chair on the ground. Feel the energy passing from the ground into your body.

Step Five:

Finally, very slowly move your awareness to the sky and then down again to the ground. Imagine an energy force connecting the sky and the ground, and feel yourself infused with the energy of both. Remain in this state of awareness for as long as you feel comfortable, and then conclude the exercise with some slowly, rhythmic breathing.

Slowly open your eyes, but remain seated for a few moments, allowing your mind to completely recover.

Conclusion

As well as intending my story to be a psychological process, primarily for myself, I had also hoped that it would allow you to see that the power of the spirit is greater than any wrong you may have done, and that no matter how old you are, it is never too late to change. It is all too easy to allow yourself to be pulled along by circumstances, but there is always an inner voice calling for you to break free. It's not always easy to listen to this inner voice particularly when circumstances very frequently dictate all the rules. Over the years I have learned not to compare myself to others, and never to allow others to influence me to go against that inner voice. I know that I have lived many, many times before; but even in this life, like you, I have had numerous incarnations. I intend now to make the best of who and what I am!

Since this book was finished I have secured a contract to do a television commercial for Nokia mobiles. I'm quite pleased about this as I know it's just another pathway upon which to walk.

www.apexpublishing.co.uk